CHRISTMAS
TRADITIONS

from the heart

By Margaret Peters

To Sally
With Christmas Joy!
Margaret Peters

C&T PUBLISHING

Copyright © 1992 Margaret Peters

Edited by Harold Nadel

Technical information edited by Elizabeth Aneloski and Janet Macik Myers

Recipes edited by Elizabeth Aneloski, Cathy Miller, and Sheila Pedersen

Design and electronic illustrations by "Rose Sheifer Graphic Productions"
Walnut Creek, California

Photography by Sharon Risedorph, San Francisco, California

Cover photograph by Barnett Photography, Danville, California

Room styling assistance by Candy MacPherson

Twig chair courtesy of Eleanor Broyles, Homestead, Napa, California

Published by C & T Publishing
P. O. Box 1456
Lafayette, California 94549

ISBN 0-914881-48-5

Library of Congress Cataloging-in-Publication Data

Peters, Margaret. 1931–
     Christmas traditions from the heart / by Margaret Peters : [edited by Harold Nadel]. — 1st ed.
          p.   cm.
     ISBN 0-914881-48-5
     1. Christmas decorations.   2. Patchwork—Patterns.   3. Christmas cookery.
     I. Nadel, Harold.   II. Title.
     TT900. C4P455   1992
     745.594 ' 12—dc20   92–71399
                                                                         CIP

Printed in Hong Kong
10 9 8 7 6 5 4 3 2 1

TABLE OF CONTENTS

This book is dedicated to Jean Wells, Harold Nadel, and Carolie Hensley, for their encouragement, wisdom, and friendship; to Michael Kile, who said, "You do it!"; and, above all, to my dear husband, Pete, who held the ladder while I reached for my star, and to our children, Mary and Dianne, Dirk and Scott, for precious memories—I love you all.

As the cold weather of December draws close upon us (yes, even in California, relatively), most of us bundle up to brave the chill and the crowds, to begin our Christmas shopping. Only most of us, for quilters and sewers may start a creative project on Christmas evening for the next year's giving, or may start a different project just a few days before Christmas.

In my life I have been blessed with many treasured friends, talented in their unique ways. All of us have been given gifts which will be remembered through the years as special, whether quilts, art-to-wear garments, dolls, teddy bears, or a memorable table setting or dinner. In this book, some of my dear friends have joined with me to share their talents, traditions, artistic secrets, recipes, and love of the season with you.

I have invited the designers to tell you exactly how they create their projects. You should realize, though, that the particular brands they mention are only suggestions; other manufacturers offer products which are just as good, and which will work just as well for you. Feel free to let your shopkeeper recommend alternative brands.

Margaret Peters: Bundle of Love

Color picture on page 50

In the course of my life I have been blessed with many wonderful people and experiences. There is the excitement and joy of my life with my professional football player husband and my four children. Life already seemed full, but much was to change in 1987.

I have always loved creating and teaching crafts. In 1986 I designed an angel ornament for a Christmas gift exchange for a group of friends. Pete, my husband, Marinda Stewart, and Karen Drellich, building upon the fact that I had been frightened away from an offer several years earlier to decorate a tree for the Smithsonian Institution, persuaded me now to send my Patriotic Angel to Washington: as a result, I was invited again to do a tree, to be placed at the foot of the flag which inspired Francis Scott Key to write "The Star-Spangled Banner." From that start grew my own company, and my travels around the country lecturing on the meaning of being an American.

If those three dear people had not pushed me, I would have missed out on the most thrilling times of my life. I had always taught my children to reach for their own stars, and one of my sons chided me for not following my own advice when I resisted sending the angel. Now one Smithsonian angel is in The White House, at Barbara Bush's request — and I am writing this book!

With all of the wonders and excitement in life, we must be careful not to rush so quickly that we miss the path that will change the entire course of our lives. We need the people around us who prod and encourage us from their love and faith in us. I thank and love them, and I encourage you, too, to reach for your star.

The other fact of my life which led me to this book is the importance of Christmas in my life. In the midst of the dark of winter, the lights and joy of Christmas brighten our hearts and re-awaken the children in us. I make my home as welcoming at this season as the shop windows downtown.

On my living-room mantel are eighty Santas, looking out over at least two trees and at least twenty teddy bears working frantically to get their projects done. They are arranged in a theme each year, decorating the trees or wrapping packages or making cookies. When my grandchildren get up Christmas morning, they can see that the dolls have been working all night. They also see Santa's big, ashy footprints across the rug, from the fireplace to the tree; he has left a mountain of gifts and a note of thanks for the cookies and milk, and the carrots for his reindeer. Every room in the house is decorated, even the bathrooms, a task that fills us with memories of Christmases past, from our childhoods and down to our seven grandchildren.

Setting up the crèche is always a special time for me, to tell the children the story of what took place in that stable so long ago, to see the wonder in their eyes when they hear that no one would provide a room for the new baby. I put my Bible next to the crèche, opened to the second chapter of Luke, the first twenty verses underlined in red. Be sure to give yourself the thrill of hearing your own child or grandchild read the story aloud!

A few years ago, at Thanksgiving, I gave each of our adult children a small bag containing the name of a brother or sister. They were to take it home, write their favorite memory of that person, and put it in the bag. At Christmas morning breakfast, they read what they have written; the little bags are then hung on the tree, and brought out again each year. How I treasure those thoughts!

I also have a Christmas box with small wind-up toys, brought out only at Christmas. This year my daughter-in-law Peggy also began a similar box with her own children. When our children were at home, I would waken them each morning from December first with Christmas records: as a gift to myself, that was the only music allowed in the living room during the entire month — and that rule still holds today. Christmas is for children, and I love to have this annual chance to become child-like once more in the wonder and glory of the season. In the words of one of my Christmastime helpers, "Merry Christmas to all, and to all a good night!"

MATERIALS

- ⅝ yard of outer fabric
- ⅝ yard of lining fabric
- ½ yard for contrast flaps
- (If you prefer to use only one fabric, you will need a total of 2 yards.)
- Allow extra fabric for matching up plaids, large prints, or one-way designs.
- 2 yards of ½"-wide satin ribbon
- 1½ yards of novelty braid or 1¼"-wide ribbon
- 1¾ yards of pre-gathered lace or eyelet trim

- 18" × 44" piece of 10-ounce batting
- Matching thread
- Perle cotton #3 contrast color for tying the bundle

CUTTING

- Cut two pieces 18" × 44" each for back and lining.
- Cut two pieces 21" × 14½" for the flaps.
- Cut satin ribbon into 4 pieces, each 18" long.
- Cut braid into 4 pieces, each 11" long.

ASSEMBLY

1. Lay the back and lining pieces right sides together and baste or pin. Fold in half, long sides together, and cut edges even. Cut a curve 3" down: I measure 3" down on the cut edge, then place one edge of a saucer at this point and place the saucer to meet the top edge, draw a line and cut.

2. Fold one of the 21" × 14½" pieces, right sides together, to make a piece 10½" × 14½". Stitch across the 10½" sides, with a ½" seam allowance. Clip the corners and turn right side out. Repeat for the other flap.

3. Fold under one end of each piece of braid ½" to make a clean edge, and baste.

4. Lay braids 3" from the top and 3" from the bottom of the flaps, as shown, and sew along the edge of the braid. Then sew ⅜" in from each long edge of the braid to create a casing for the ribbon. Put a safety pin in one end of a ribbon and run the ribbon through a casing, pulling about ¼" of ribbon beyond the casing on the raw edge.

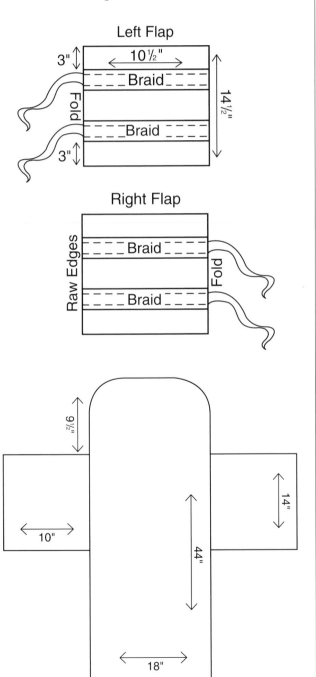

5. Place the flaps inside the outer fabric and lining, with the top of the flap 9½" down from the top. Be sure the ribbon side faces the back. Pin or baste; then, starting ½" up from the bottom, stitch up one side, across the top, and down the other side, catching the flaps in; stop ½" from the bottom. Turn right side out and press.

6. Sew gathered lace or eyelet trim across the top edge, turning the raw edges of the trim under at both ends.

7. Put the batting inside. Along the bottom edge, fold ½" seam allowance to inside, and stitch across. Add eyelet lace across the back bottom edge on the outside of the back, so it will show when the bundle is folded up.

8. With perle cotton, tie the layers together, 2½" from the top and centered. Then go down 4" and make two ties, 4" in from the sides. Then make another single tie, down another 4".

9. Fold the bottom up so that it is 2"-3" above the flaps. Pull the ribbons tight and tie in bows, gathering the flaps in.

10. Take the bundle to the new mother in the hospital, ready to bring home her bundle of joy in her Bundle of Love.

If you are making this for a baby boy, you may prefer to use piping, cording, or pleated edging instead of lace.

The Bundle of Love takes less than two hours to make; thus far, I have made about three dozen, no two alike. Mothers and grandmothers love them, as the babies cannot kick the bundles off!

On the day we photographed the cover of this book at my house, I wanted to serve something to the huddled masses that could be prepared ahead and get better waiting for us. This Taco Soup filled the bill successfully, and was such a hit that the editor insisted I present it to you here. So, Harold, dear friend, this one is for you. It is a great recipe for those cold nights, and for your holiday season drop-in guests: you'll have most of the ingredients on hand — and only you will know which ones you might have been missing!

Taco Soup

- 1 to 1½ pounds of hamburger
- 32-ounce can of chopped tomatoes
- 16-ounce can of dark red kidney beans
- 16-ounce can of chicken broth
- 1 box of frozen corn
- 1 or 2 onions, sliced

- 1 avocado, chopped
- 1 to 2 cups of grated cheddar cheese
- 1 bag of tortilla chips
- 1 can of sliced black olives
- 1 pint of sour cream
- 1 package of taco seasoning mix

In a large soup kettle, sauté the meat until all pink is gone, breaking it up with a fork. While the meat is cooking, add the seasoning and the onions, then the tomatoes, beans (including liquid), chicken broth, and corn. (If I expect to keep this cooking for a long time, I may wait to add the corn 15 minutes before serving.) Let everything simmer slowly for a half-hour, or up to a few hours. Serve the cheese, chips, olives, and sour cream in separate bowls; the avocado should be prepared at the last moment, to prevent darkening. Serve the soup in bowls ⅔ full, then pass the toppings: chips, then cheese, sour cream, olives and avocado last. Easy, but oh so good! With a green salad and French bread, this makes a tasty and fun meal, great for a tree-trimming supper, a tailgate party, or skiing.

One of the pleasures and treats I look forward to each week is getting together with a group of very talented women each Wednesday, sharing a love of quilts and their meanings in our lives. We call ourselves the Wednesday Whiners and, at birthday and holiday occasions, the Wednesday Winers. From this group of dear friends, I have invited four to share their wonderful talents in this book — and they all loyally came through for me in less than two months! I am truly blessed to have this group of sisters who cheer each other on and give support in the scary moments.

Alex Anderson: Flying Trees

Color picture on page 51

Alex Anderson is one of the Wednesday Whiners, but she does very little whining. She is a true diamond in my life, and adds her sparkle wherever she goes. She has more energy than a roomful of six-year-olds with two buckets of toads. She has the gift of finding humor in every moment of life, and her sense of fun is infectious. But she also turns her joys and energies to her chosen tasks: devotion to her family, quilting, and teaching. Give Alex a challenge, and she is off and running and has completed the project before you've caught your breath. She has made quilts for books by Diana McClun, Laura Nownes, Mary Penders — and now, for me.

How often do we have to repeat an act to label it "tradition"? If changing times cause us to stop repeating an event, is it no longer a tradition? And if, as we often hope, our children hold special memories of the event, and revive it with their children? Of the three special Christmas traditions in our family, one is now ended — or in Limbo? We used to invite my son's friends to a special party every year: each child brought a few low-priced toys which were passed on to the Richmond Rescue Mission, for less fortunate children. A Santa provided by the fire department would spend time with each child. When my son and his friends became old enough to think it would be fun to pull off Santa's beard, we changed the guest list to my daughter's friends. The tradition ended when the girls also began to consider the pleasures of debearding.

The tradition I most want to mention here involves the same friends who go to Chinatown with us, and it takes place on the Sunday after Thanksgiving. The mothers and children have the privilege of riding in the van, while the fathers get to drive the truck — obviously, "guy stuff"! We go to a tree lot about an hour away, and we inspect each tree trying to find the Perfect One. Before we cut it down, I take a picture of my family in front of the one I have approved; some day, I will compile all the photos into a personal family document. When both families have selected and cut their trees, we load up: some day, the mothers will demand our right to drive the truck. The quilt I have made for you here reflects the emotions I feel every year as I survey the lot full of trees.

This wall hanging measures 48" × 52". Each tree unit is 4" × 5" finished size.

YARDAGE

Since this is a scrap quilt, half the fun is in looking for unusual fabrics that have textures resembling foliage and tree bark, that give the feel of dark, crisp, starry winter nights. The more variety you use, the more interesting your quilt will be. The following amounts are scrap totals in each color family.

- ¼ yard of browns for tree trunks (template D)
- 2¾ yards of blacks for background (templates B and C) and outer border strips
- 2 yards of greens (template A) (plus ½ yard of scrap fabric for the light cord, if you make your own bias strip)

- Bulbs: ⅛ yard of each of five fabrics in bright, clear colors
- ¼ yard each of reds and greens for sawtooth border
- Binding: ⅓ yard

CUTTING INSTRUCTIONS (add ¼" seam allowance)

Template A: cut 72

Template B: cut 72 rights and 72 lefts

Template C: cut 144

Template D: cut 72

Sawtooth border: cut 1⅞" strips, cut them into 1⅞" squares, then cut the squares diagonally: total of 154 triangles of each color

Outer border: 180 strips of 1½" × 5½"

Binding: five strips 2" × 44"

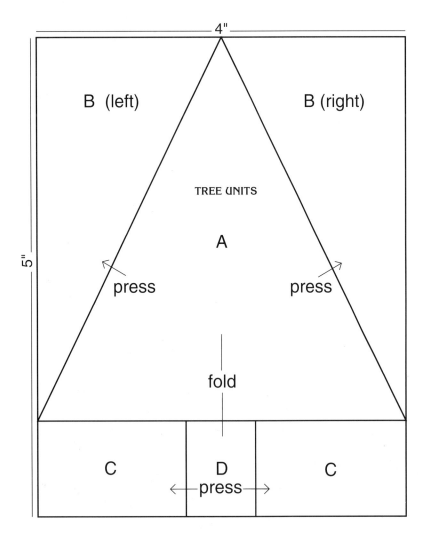

ASSEMBLY

1. To assemble the body of the tree, sew a right piece B to triangle A and press toward B; then sew a left piece B to A and press toward B.

2. To assemble the trunk section, sew a piece C to each side of D and press toward the C pieces.

3. Fold both sections vertically so the centers will match precisely, pin, and sew the trunk to the body.

4. Make 72 tree units.

5. To assemble the tree units into the quilt top, follow the illustration. The vertical rows are offset, so the odd-numbered rows have 8 trees each, and the even-numbered rows have 9 trees each.

6. After you have made the rows and stitched them together, trim off the top and bottom protrusions, so that the edges are even.

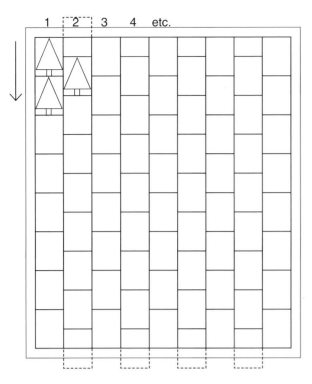

BORDERS

1. For the inner sawtooth border, you need 154 squares, each made from a red and a green half-square triangle; the finished size of each is 1" square. You also need two green squares, finished size 1" each, for the lower left and upper right corners.

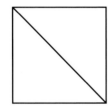

2. For each side strip, sew together a row of 40 square units. For the top, sew a row of 37 units, and attach one solid green square at the right end. For the bottom, sew a row of 37 units, and attach one solid green square at the left end. Attach these borders to the quilt top.

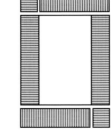

3. Press the seams toward the center of the quilt.

4. For the outer border, join the long edges of the strips into two side units of 42 strips each.

Attach one to each side of the quilt, and press toward the outer border.

5. The top and bottom outer border strips contain 48 strips each: note how the 5 corner strips have been rotated to create a continuous, intertwining clockwise motion. Attach the top and bottom strips, and press toward the outer border.

BORDER APPLIQUÉ

1. The cord is ¼" wide. You can purchase double-fold bias tape ¼" wide. You will need at least 10 yards of cord. You can make your own cord by using a bias bar: rotary cut 1"-wide bias strips, fold, and sew, using a ¼" seam allowance; insert the bias bar and press the seam under.

2. Pin the cord into place on the border.

3. Make the bulbs with an assortment of bright, clear colors. Sew strips of 3½" colored fabric to 1½" strips of a green fabric suitable for the bulb bases.

4. (I find that the easiest technique is one taught by Elly Sienkiewicz in her Baltimore appliqué books.) Cut your bulb templates from freezer paper and press them onto the fabrics, matching the fabric join line to the dotted line marked on the bulb pattern. Make about a dozen bulbs in each of five colors.

5. Cut out the bulbs, leaving a ¼" seam allowance around each bulb. Leave extra fabric below the base of each bulb, as you may need it to adjust the bulb placement.

6. To make the plug, cut a 2½" square of green fabric and a scrap of brown fabric ½" × 2½". Sew these together along the 2½" sides. Cut out the plug shape from the pattern, using freezer paper, the prongs in brown and the rest of the plug green.

7. Arrange the bulbs along the cord around the border, alternating and varying the colors. Put a bulb at one end of the cord, and the plug at the other end.

8. Appliqué, turning the edges under with a needle to maintain smooth edges on the bulb. Keep several needles threaded with colors that match the bulbs and the cord.

QUILTING

When I plan the quilting design for a scrap quilt, I like to treat the entire pieced surface as a single unit; for this quilt, I decided on an overall, free-form, random curve. I drew curves with a silver pencil, then echoed (repeated) the curve at half-inch intervals. To contain the curving movements, I quilted the border with diagonal patterns. Note that the bulbs, plug, and cord are outlined and not crossed by the diagonals, so that they float above the grid. If this approach to the quilting seems too difficult, any overall grid pattern will work well on this quilt: just be consistent with the amount of quilting on all areas.

BINDING

This type of binding does not need to be cut on the bias. Piece 2"-wide strips to a continuous 6 yards. Fold and press the strip in half lengthwise. Lay the strip along one side of the front of the quilt top, raw edges together, and attach the strip ¼" in from the edge. Cut the strip at the end of this stitching, fold it over to the back, and repeat for the other side edge. When you attach the binding strips to the top and bottom edges, leave 1" extra at each end, so you can tuck and fold to cover the raw edges of the side bindings. You will have a ¼" finished binding all around the quilt.

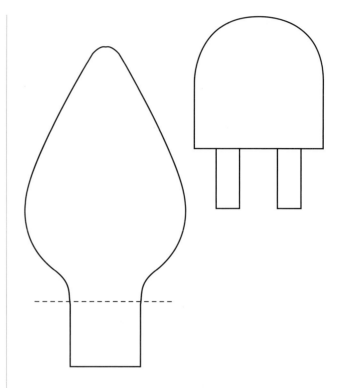

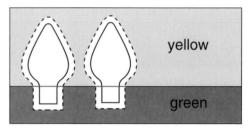

yellow

green

Christmas Day at our house includes a special late-afternoon meal, after the excitement of opening presents all morning. I have little energy left for an elaborate menu, so the crowd-pleasing menu contains ham, vegetables, and...

The World's Best Scalloped Potatoes

- 6 to 8 medium potatoes
- 2 medium onions
- 2 cans of cream of mushroom soup
- 1 soup can of milk
- ½ pound of grated colby cheese
- ½ pound of grated pepper jack cheese

Oil a 3-quart casserole with a lid. Peel the potatoes and onions, and slice them thin. Layer half the potatoes, half the onions, half the cheese in the casserole, and repeat. Mix the soup and milk and pour on top. Bake at 325° covered for one hour and uncovered for another hour, until golden on top. Serves 10-12 hungry celebrants.

Sally Collins: Oh Christmas Tree

Color picture on page 52

Another of the Wednesday Whiners is Sally Collins, who is also my neighbor. She teaches throughout the area, and she has her own pattern company. Sally's specialty is miniature quilts; many of her quilt squares are three inches or less! Sally is one of the best teachers I have ever studied with; she is also the one who gave the group its name, since we whined so much in class when she had us working with half-inch pieces. However, with her discipline and loving kindness, we all finished our little quilts. She says she turned to miniature quilts because she ran out of wall space at home; she also makes tiny room shadow boxes, each with a wee quilt hanging on its wall.

I wanted to make a quilt with simple construction, offering an opportunity to experiment with many different fabrics within a controlled color scheme. Although this quilt uses only reds, greens, and off-whites, I used 21 different greens for the tree and 22 different background fabrics. The varied values and visual textures impart a faceted, mottled look that adds depth and richness. I selected a deep, rich red for the curved border, then a narrow black border, and finally a border of a green plaid used in the tree. The stars add bright yellow, purple, red, blue, green, orange, and fuchsia. The appliquéd bow is in different reds, outlined and defined by black embroidery thread.

Finished size is 35" × 38". Use ¼" seam allowance throughout. Read all instructions before beginning. The quilt is based on a 3" grid with each square divided diagonally into quarters. The diagram does not show the narrow border or final border.

FABRIC REQUIRED

I recommend that you use 100% cottons throughout. Note that you will also be using muslin border strips, for stabilizing the curved pieces.

- Stars: scraps
- Background: assorted fabrics to total ½ yard
- Tree: assorted fabrics to total ½ yard
- Curved border: 1 yard
- Narrow border: ⅛ yard
- Final border: ⅓ yard
- Batting: 40" × 42"
- Backing: 40" × 42"

ASSEMBLY

1. Cut a wide assortment of shades, values, and visual textures of greens and background fabrics into 4¼" squares, then cut each square diagonally into four triangles.

2. On a fleece surface, and referring to the diagram, place the triangles to form the tree and background. When you are satisfied with the placement, sew the triangles together to form squares.

3. Seven of the 3" squares are 3" sawtooth stars with central 1½" sawtooth stars. I made the 3" stars from background fabrics, and the 1½" stars from bright, clear colors which would really show up and twinkle. Sew the stars as instructed and place them appropriately, according to the diagram.

Large Star

3" finished size

FOR EACH STAR

- Cut four 1¼" squares of background fabric.
- Cut four 1¼" × 2" rectangles of background fabric.
- Cut eight 1¼" squares of star fabric.

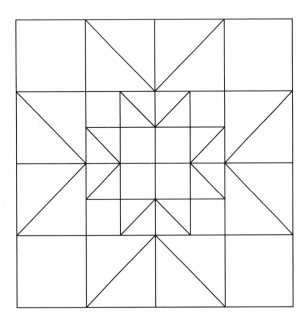

Small Star

1½" finished size

FOR EACH STAR

- Cut four ⅞" squares of background fabric.
- Cut four ⅞" × 1¼" rectangles of background fabric.
- Cut eight ⅞" squares of star fabric.
- Cut one 1¼" square of central star fabric.

Assembly for Both Stars

1. Mark a diagonal line on the wrong side of eight ⅞" and eight 1¼" star fabric squares: this is your sewing line.

2. Following the diagram, sew star squares to background rectangles. The units formed are your star points. Trim after sewing each square onto the rectangle, and press to the star point.

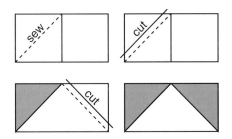

3. Place the star points, background squares, and center star as shown to form the completed star. Sew into rows, then sew the rows together, matching the intersections and pinning as needed to complete the block.

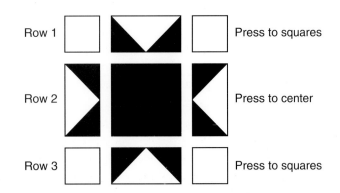

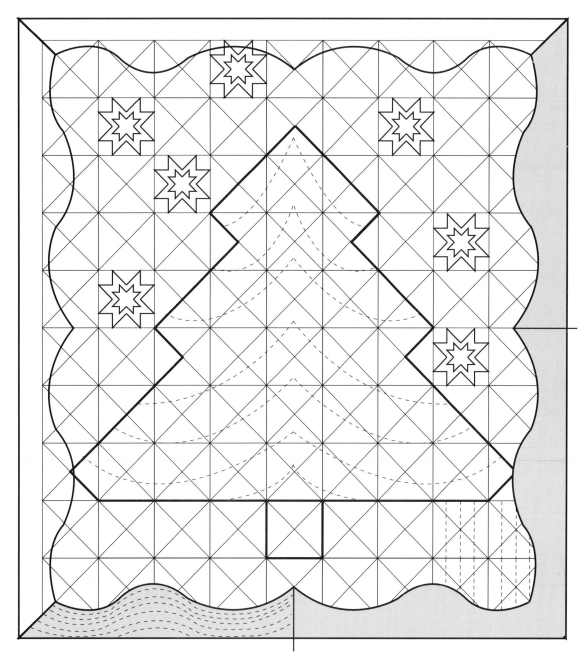

4. Sew the squares together to form horizontal rows.

5. Join the rows together, matching the intersections, to form the body of the quilt.

6. Add a 1¾" × 30" muslin border strip to each of the two sides and press. Then add a 2" × 30" muslin strip to the top, and one to the bottom, and press. The quilt should now measure 30" × 33".

7. Following the diagram, draw (full size) on graph paper the curved edge, from bottom center to the center of the right side. Cut this out for your template for one quarter of the quilt top.

8. Cut a rectangle 30" x 33" from the fabric you've chosen for the curved border. Fold it in half, then half again, to determine the center point and the centers of the sides. Mark the center points. Pin the paper template in place, mark the curved line, and repeat for the other three sides.

9. Place the marked rectangle on top of the quilt, right side up, matching and pinning the centers of the sides. Baste securely from the outside edge to the marked line.

10. Cut away the center, ¼" from the marked line outside the finished shape. After removing the center piece, you will have your ¼" seam allowance.

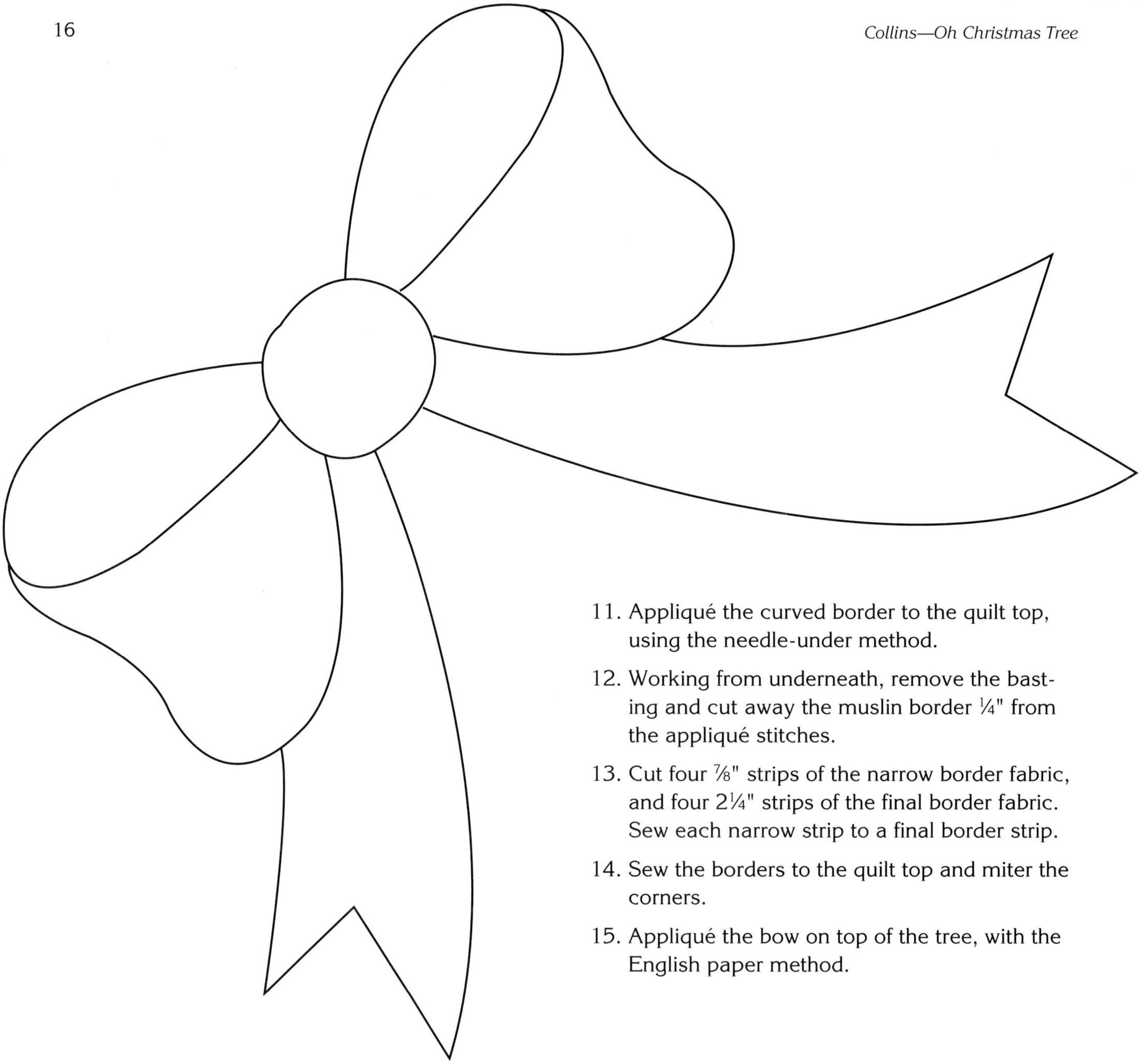

11. Appliqué the curved border to the quilt top, using the needle-under method.

12. Working from underneath, remove the basting and cut away the muslin border ¼" from the appliqué stitches.

13. Cut four ⅞" strips of the narrow border fabric, and four 2¼" strips of the final border fabric. Sew each narrow strip to a final border strip.

14. Sew the borders to the quilt top and miter the corners.

15. Appliqué the bow on top of the tree, with the English paper method.

Pecan Sandies

- 1 cup of softened butter
- ⅓ cup of sugar
- 2 teaspoons of water
- 2 teaspoons of vanilla extract
- 2 cups of sifted flour
- 1 cup of chopped nuts

Cream the butter and sugar together, add water and vanilla, mix well. Add the flour and nuts and mix well. Chill two hours. Shape into small balls and bake on an ungreased cookie sheet, at 325°, for 20 minutes. Cool slightly, then roll the cookies in powdered sugar, or sift powdered sugar over them.

Anna Judd Edwards: Peace on Earth

Color picture on page 53

Anna Edwards is the ballast of the Wednesday Whiners: she keeps us on course with her serenity and her extensive quilting knowledge, which grows daily. She views everything she does as a challenge to be met and enriched. Her love of her family and devotion to them spills over every Wednesday to include all of us. I knew the quilt she would design for this book would be wonderful, but I had no idea how wonderful until I saw what she has given us.

This quilt was a joy for me to make: I wanted it to be a Christmas card that need not be opened to display its message. I share my wish for Peace on Earth with all of you.

Although there are many methods for appliqué, I have used the needle-turn method almost throughout this quilt. I used reverse appliqué to attach the background fabric to the picture oval, as well as for the banner message and the whites of the lion's eyes.

This large appliqué work is most easily approached as a set of units. This concept is especially useful when some pieces are attached only partially until another unit is added. For example, one of the angel's fingers overlaps the bird, and must be finished after the bird is in place. Once a unit has been appliquéd to its foundation, be sure to cut away excess foundation fabric from the back, to lighten the bulk: cut very carefully to about ¼" of the stitch lines.

Pattern marking and placement are done most easily with a light box. Mark all pattern pieces on the right side of the fabric, just outside of the pattern piece line, allowing a ¼" seam allowance. Because you will using needle turning, the marked line will be turned under and hidden.

Start with a 40" square for the background fabric: you can trim away the excess edges later. Fold the fabric into quarters and press, so you will have an accurate center point and guidelines for matching the fabric with the pattern. Mark the reference crosses and the oval (just inside the marking line) on the fabric first, using a silver pencil.

Enlarge the pattern, inserted at the back of the book, 180%.

FABRIC REQUIRED

I have used 100% cottons. I prewashed only those which might bleed or fade. Yardages given are based upon the minimum cut at most fabric stores. If you have suitable small pieces from other projects, use the approximate sizes given in parentheses.

Oval

BACKGROUND FABRICS

- Sky: ½ yard (16" × 21")
- Far hill: ⅛ yard (3" × 8")
- Center: ½ yard (10" × 22")
- Foreground: ½ yard (11" × 22")

TREES

- Three trees: ¼ yard

ANGEL

- Wings: ⅓ yard (12"× 14")
- Hair: ⅛ yard (4" × 5")
- Face, hands, and foot: ⅛ yard (6" × 6")
- Dress: ¼ yard
- Embroidery floss: black (lashes), beige (brow and nose), rose (lips), blue (eye), gold metallic thread (halo)

DOVE

- Body: ⅛ yard (4" × 4")
- Embroidery floss: golden (feet and beak), black (eye), dark green (branch)

LAMB

- Face and hooves: ⅛ yard (4" × 4")
- Body and ear: ¼ yard (8" × 8")
- Embroidery floss: light gray (outline, mouth, and eyelid)

LION

- Body, paws, and face: ⅛ yard
- Nose and mouth: ⅛ yard (3" × 3")
- Muzzle: ⅛ yard (4" × 4")
- Mane: ¼ yard (8" × 8")
- Embroidery floss: lime green and black (eyes), brown (claws and whiskers)

OVERALL BACKGROUND

- 1¼ yards

BANNER

- Lettering: ⅛ yard
- Banner: ¼ and ⅛ yards

HOLLY WREATH

- Woody vine: ⅛ yard
- Leaves: ⅛ yard each of half a dozen different fabrics

- Berries: ⅛ yard each of two fabrics

BORDER

The borders were made from a print which had repeat linear strips. Four strips were cut to 6" × 1½ yards, which provide extra length for mitering the corners. Using a border fabric allows you to follow the printed design for the quilting, adding an exciting texture.

BACKING

- 48" × 50"

BATTING

- 48" × 50" of low-loft polyester or cotton-polyester blend

ASSEMBLY

Unit 1: Oval

As you are marking the background oval picture unit, extend the sky and ground lines beyond the oval. This will make it easier to reverse appliqué the background fabric to the oval unit. Starting with the background scenery, mark the reference crosses with the silver pencil. Next, carefully mark the placement of the pattern pieces onto the scenery. Mark lightly ¼" inside the pattern pieces, to allow for shifting. These markings will be hidden by the appliquéd pieces. I use a mechanical pencil to mark very fine placement lines. Appliqué the trees to the background scenery.

Unit 2: Angel

Appliqué in the following order: wings, face and throat, hands (remember that part of the right hand overlaps the bird), left sleeve, dress, right sleeve, hair. With a single strand of embroidery floss of appropriate color, embroider the eyebrow, lashes, eye (French knot), nostril (tiny French knot), and lip definition (single stitch). The halo is made with gold metallic thread: make a small running stitch, then come back under the running stitches with the eye of the needle still threaded, weaving in and out through the stitches, to make a solid line.

Unit 3: Lion

Appliqué in the following order: body, paws, mane, face. The face is actually a separate unit with appliquéd mouth, nose, and muzzle attached to the face piece. Reverse appliqué the white of the eyes. Appliqué the face to the mane and embellish it with embroidered eye details, whiskers, and claws.

Unit 4: Bird

Appliqué the bird's body, then the wing. Embroider the beak, eye, feet, and olive branch.

Unit 5: Lamb

Appliqué the lamb's body to the face, the body fabric on top, then the ear to the head. Embroider the eye and the mouth. Then appliqué the lamb to the quilt, and attach the hooves.

At this point, the scenery is complete. Now, place the background fabric over the scene, both face up, and align the reference crosses. Pin in place, and baste carefully ½" inside and outside of the oval, to prevent the pieces from shifting while you are reverse appliquéing the background fabric onto the scene. Please work slowly and accurately. Cut carefully ¼" inside of the marked oval a few inches at a time as you needle-turn the top fabric to the scene below. You now have an oval picture, ready for the next units. Place this over the master pattern, and carefully mark a fine line for the placement of the vine. Mark the center vein of each leaf, and a dot for each berry.

Unit 6: Banner

The lettering must be marked onto the front of the fabric. Lay the lettering fabric face up beneath the banner fabric. Baste the fabrics together to prevent shifting. Reverse appliqué, cutting away from the front while turning the edges under. The stitches must be small, so work slowly. The banner side pieces also must be treated gently: they are cut with bias edges and can stretch out of shape easily. Be sure to keep banner ends open for the overlapped leaves: refer to the master pattern for the appliqué order here.

Unit 7: Holly Wreath

Appliqué in the following order: stems, leaves, berries.

LAYERING AND QUILTING

Add the borders, mitering the corners. Put the three layers — top, batting, backing — together and quilt. For the border, see my comments above about quilting around the design. For the central appliqué, you will probably want to quilt in the lines around the appliquéd pieces. Then, either use the photograph as a guide to other quilting designs I selected for the backgrounds and the figures, or make your own quilting decisions.

BINDING

Using a rotary cutter, cut six strips 2" × 44" each and sew them together end to end with a diagonal seam, pressed open. Then fold the strip in half lengthwise, wrong sides together, and press. Before attaching the binding, trim any excess backing, batting, and border. Place the binding on the front side of the quilt, raw edges of binding and quilt together. Leaving a few inches of binding free, start stitching a few inches beyond a corner, with a ¼" seam allowance. Stop ¼" before the next corner, backstitch a few stitches and clip the thread. At the corner, fold the binding up and away, creating a 45° angle. Fold the binding back toward the next side of the quilt to create a right-angle tuck at the corner. Begin sewing again with a ¼" seam allowance on the second side. Repeat this technique for the next two corners. When you reach the starting corner, overlap the excess from the starting end of the binding with a piece from the finishing end, enough to blind-stitch the ends together. Sew down the joined binding. Then fold the binding to the back of the quilt and blind-stitch the binding to the quilt.

I know you had as much fun making this quilt as I did. You, your family, and your guests will enjoy your finished creation for many years to come. And don't forget to label your quilt with your name, the date, the occasion, etc.

Georgia Fruit Cake

All ingredients should be at room temperature.

Combine

- 4 cups of flour
- 1 teaspoon of baking powder
- 1 teaspoon of salt
- 1 tablespoon each of nutmeg, cinnamon, allspice, and ground cloves

Toss 1 cup of the mixture with the following to coat:

- 1 cup of chopped dates
- 4 cups of coarsely chopped pecans
- 2 cups of washed and drained currants
- 3 cups of candied fruits
- 1 cup of white raisins
- (optional) some chopped dried apricots

Cream together 1 pound of butter with 2½ cups of brown sugar. Add some orange zest, a tablespoon of vanilla extract, and ½ cup of thick orange juice or orange liqueur. Slowly and alternately stir in the dry mixture and 12 large eggs. Fold in the fruit-nut mixture.

Pour the batter into a lightly greased Bundt pan and a loaf pan. Bake at 275° for three to three and a half hours. If you prefer to put all of the batter into one pan, you will have to increase the baking time and test with a toothpick to be sure the cake is done.

When the cakes have cooled partially, remove them from the pans. Wrap each cake in cheesecloth and drench them with brandy, orange liqueur, or non-alcoholic sherry. Place them in airtight containers in the refrigerator for two weeks, checking to see if they need any additional liquid. Then let them air-dry for at least ten minutes before cutting.

Rosalee Sanders:
'Twas The Night Before Christmas

Color picture on page 54

Rosalee Sanders is a very cherished friend, and the hostess of the weekly gatherings. Her extra-special gift is her quilting stitch: when she finished this quilt, she discovered that her hand-quilting stitch was the same size as the stitch in her Bernina machine. Her quilts have appeared in books and magazines, but her biggest challenge so far has been in teaching me to quilt, especially in a hoop: "You will," said she. And I have never heard her whine about the mess we leave in her house every Wednesday.

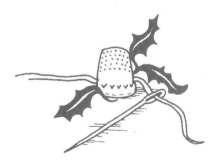

The quilting community has very definitely become my extended family, and especially a small group I belong to. There are seven of us, and for years we have drawn names for a Christmas gift exchange. Two years ago, we decided that the gift should be a wall-hanging-size quilt. That year, after we exchanged our gifts, we shared our thoughts about making the quilts. At first, we all had viewed it as a commitment to be gotten out of the way; however, as we went through the steps of choosing patterns and fabrics with the recipient in mind, and then the actual construction and quilting, a special bonding developed with the person for whom we were making the quilt. I know that I personally thought of the friend each time I worked on the quilt, of the many wonderful shared moments which I had not thought of in so long. Often, I find it difficult to let go of a quilt once it is finished; this time, I couldn't wait for the joy of presenting it to my friend.

Because of that first experience, this past year I made quilts for two very special people in my life, and they were joyful times. Each quilt was very different and, I hope, expressed my love for the friend. Making the quilts for specific and beloved people made it very easy to give them up when the time came. I am sure that the recipients are enjoying the quilts — and I had the joy of making them, and of making our friendships just that much more special. I don't expect to be able to do this every year, but I am very glad that I decided to do it this year. The experience made my Christmas!

In order to make this quilt, you must first transfer the design to the fabric you have chosen for the quilt top. You may wish to work directly from the pattern in the book, or you may prefer to make a working copy of the pattern. To make a copy, use lightweight white paper or tracing paper, and tape the pieces together so that you will have a large enough sheet for the complete pattern.

If you are working with light-colored fabric, I strongly advise that you use a quilter's mechanical pencil: it creates a very fine line which washes out thoroughly, disappears as you quilt over it, and can be erased. (Be careful, though: ironing makes the pencil lines permanent!) If you are working on a dark table, first cover it with white paper. Tape the pattern firmly to the table, lay the fabric over the pattern, carefully matching the center point and other guidelines, and trace carefully with the pencil.

On dark fabrics, I use dressmaker's carbon — but I always pre-test to be sure that it will wash out of the fabric. I do not recommend other marking techniques: ink may leave a residue, and pouncing, chalk, and soap wear off too quickly when you are working on so large a piece. Tape the fabric tautly to the table, cover it with the carbon paper in a slightly contrasting color, and cover this with the pattern sheet. Match up all of the guidelines carefully, and tape all layers securely. Run a tracing wheel or a ball-point pen over the marked lines, re-positioning the carbon paper as necessary.

After the pattern has been transferred to the fabric, you are ready to put your quilt layers together. I used the thinnest batting I could find, an ultra-low-loft; I never use cotton batting, as it beards and the needle drags. I use either a #10 or #12 quilting needle, with a thimble. Baste the quilt top, batting, and backing together on a 4" square grid, and insert the sandwich into your quilting hoop or frame. I suggest a fairly tight tension, to help you make smaller stitches. Personally, I do not like the stiffness of machine-quilted whole-cloth quilts, so I advise you to quilt this by hand. Do not attempt to quilt with more than 18" of thread at a time, or you run the risk of fraying. If you are not using quilting thread, wax your regular thread. Work outward from the center of the quilt; be careful that both the top and the backing remain smooth. You can quilt the background as a grid, or with stipple quilting; add stars, chimney, or other Christmas motifs you like. I sometimes use a border design to frame the entire quilt. Be inventive!

The finished size of this quilt is 34½" × 45".

Enlarge the pattern, inserted at the back of the book, 120%.

Cranberry Salad

In a food grinder (NOT a processor), coarsely grind 2 unpeeled oranges and 1 quart of fresh cranberries. Add 2 cups of sugar and simmer for 2 minutes. Add 2 small packages of lemon gelatin dissolved in ½ cup of hot water, as well as 1 cup of chopped walnuts and 1 cup of chopped celery. Pour in a mold and chill until set.

 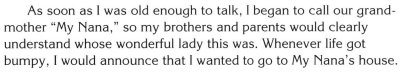
Color picture on page 55

Rhondi Hindman has been my friend for more than a decade: she taught the first class I took on making quilted garments. She also teaches one of the most popular classes in the area, an all-nighter from 9 p.m. to 7 a.m. It always has a waiting list, since so much gets accomplished, and Rhondi's perkiness keeps the fun level high. Many of her quilts have appeared in print, one of her garments was in the Cut From the Same Cloth show, she teaches regularly three times a week, and she makes samples for the quilting shop she works at. She must be sleeping sometime, to judge from her energy and infectious humor!

As soon as I was old enough to talk, I began to call our grandmother "My Nana," so my brothers and parents would clearly understand whose wonderful lady this was. Whenever life got bumpy, I would announce that I wanted to go to My Nana's house.

And it was at her house that our sugar cookie tradition began. Each year, before Christmas, My Nana would get the shortening and sugar ready, and then let me sift the flour — all over the kitchen and me. After all the ingredients finally made it into the bowl, she would let me use my generously floured hands to knead the dough. After she rolled it out, I would sit on the counter and use the same cookie cutters that I use today to cut out Nana's Sugar Cookies.

My Nana is gone now, but she did live long enough to make sugar cookies with my daughter Melissa, who so lovingly called her great-grandmother My Nana. Melissa is twelve now, and she helps me continue the tradition of making Nana's Sugar Cookies.

The finished size is 44" × 50½".

MATERIALS

- Olfa® cutter, mat, and acrylic ruler
- Fabric scissors
- 1 yard of paper-backed fusible webbing
- Black permanent-ink fine-tipped pen
- Neutral-colored thread
- Cookie cutters
- ½ yard of striped fabric (A)
- ½ yard of light print fabric (B)
- ½ yard of green or dark print fabric (C)
- ⅔ yard of light background fabric (D)
- ⅓ yard of inner-border fabric
- ½ yard of outer-border fabric
- 10-12 different Christmas fabrics (6" squares)

Cut all fabric from selvage to selvage.

ASSEMBLY

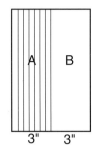

1. From fabrics A and B, cut four strips 3" x 44" (width of fabric) each. Sew each A strip to a B strip to make four sets.

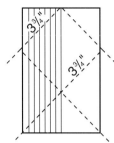

2. With your ruler, cut these strips diagonally into 3¾" squares. Cut 30 of these half-square triangles.

3. Cut three 3¾" strips of fabric C, and cut them into 3¾" squares.

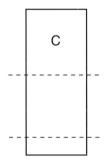 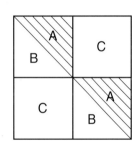

4. Sew fifteen four-patch squares. Each square will measure 7".

5. Cut 3 strips of background fabric D, 7" × 44". Cut these into 15 squares.

6. Starting with a background square, and alternating background with four-patches, sew the squares together. The quilt is five squares across and six squares down.

7. To make the inner border, cut four strips 2½" × 44" each. Cut two of the strips 39½" long and attach them to the sides of the quilt top. Cut the other strips to 37" long and add them to the top and bottom.

8. For the outer border, cut four strips 4" × 44" each. Cut two strips to 43½" inches for the sides and attach them; add the 44" strips to top and bottom.

9. Now you are ready for the cookies. With your cookie cutters, trace shapes onto the smooth side of the paper-backed fusible webbing. Place these templates webbing side down onto the wrong side of the fabric and press according to the manufacturer's directions. Cut on the traced lines with scissors, remove the paper backing, and place the designs on the background. Press according to the manufacturer's instructions.

10. You may machine appliqué, hand feather stitch, or machine quilt these designs.

11. Finish the quilt by tying or quilting it.

Nana's Sugar Cookies

- 2¼ cups of sifted flour
- ¼ teaspoon of salt
- 2 teaspoons of baking powder
- ½ cup of shortening
- 1 cup of granulated sugar

- 2 eggs, beaten
- ¾ teaspoon of vanilla extract
- 1 tablespoon of nutmeg
- 1 tablespoon of milk

Sift flour, salt, and baking powder together. Cream shortening and sugar together, add eggs, vanilla, and nutmeg, then add the sifted ingredients and milk. Flour a cutting surface and knead the dough, sprinkling it with flour several times as necessary. Roll it out and cut into shapes with cookie cutters. Bake the cookies on an ungreased baking sheet at 375° for 10-12 minutes. The recipe makes about 30 cookies.

Claire Jarratt: Double Nine-Patch

Color picture on page 56

Claire Jarratt has been my friend for a quarter-century. Whenever I am with her, I envy her calm nature and gentle ways. She is a lover of nature and always alert to her surroundings. Her love of gardening and flowers comes through in all of her work. I once took a class from her which focussed on black and white, and still everything she designed reflected her love of nature. She is an artist with needle and spade. To have her share two of her designs with me is a real compliment.

YARDAGE

The finished size of the quilt is 60" × 73".

- 3½ yards of muslin for nine-patches and alternate blocks
- 5 pieces ¼ yard each of red print fabrics for nine-patches
- ¼ yard of solid red fabric for berries
- 2 yards of green print fabric for leaves, corner blocks, ⅜" border, and ⅜" binding
- ⅓ yard of brown fabric for stems
- 5 yards of backing fabric
- 64" × 77" of batting

ASSEMBLY

1. Make 100 nine-patch blocks of reds and muslin, using 1½" squares to make 3½" blocks. You will use 400 muslin squares and 500 red squares.

2. Join these with plain muslin 3½" squares to make 20 double nine-patch blocks, each 9" square finished size.

3. You will also need 12 alternate muslin blocks 9½" square. Six will be left plain, and six will be appliquéd.

4. To appliqué the six holly blocks, cut the fabric to the size of the pattern pieces for machine appliqué. For hand appliqué, add ¼" seam allowance. All the leaves are cut from the same green print, and all of the holly berries are the same size. Use whatever method of appliqué you most prefer.

5. The stems are made from ¼" brown bias binding. Cut 1"-wide bias strips, fold, and sew, using a ¼" seam allowance. You can use Celtic bias bars to shape them, or be more creatively free-form.

6. (Optional) After the appliqué is done, chain stitch embroidered center spines on the leaves.

7. The alternate plain muslin squares will be quilted later, using the suggested quilting design given.

8. Assemble the quilt top, following the placement shown for the nine-patches, appliquéd and solid squares. First make diagonal rows. Then, you will need triangles for the edges and corners. For the edges, make 14 half-square triangles from 9⅞" muslin squares cut in half diagonally; for the corners, make a 10⅜" square, then cut it diagonally in both directions for the four quarter-square triangles. Attach all the triangles to the rows, again referring to the placement drawing.

9. The small green border is ½"–wide. Cut six 1" strips from the green print and seam them into one long strip. Cut two 51" lengths and attach them to the top and bottom of the quilt. Cut two 65" lengths and attach them to the sides of the quilt.

10. To make the main border, which is 4½" wide, cut six 5" strips of muslin and seam them into one long strip. Cut it into two 52½" strips and two 65" strips. Add the shorter pieces to the top and bottom of the quilt. Thecorner posts are small double nine-patches. In order to make the corners, make 20 nine-patches from 1" squares (80 green and 100 red), then join them with 2" muslin squares to make four blocks, each 5" square. Add a block to each end of each 65" strip of muslin, and attach these to the sides of the quilt.

11. Appliqué holly leaves, berries, and vines onto the border, in your own pattern, or following mine.

12. The binding is ⅜" wide. Cut six 1" strips and seam them into one long strip.

13. You now can do all the quilting in the plain blocks, and overall. For the overall quilting design, I used a ¾" crosshatch grid.

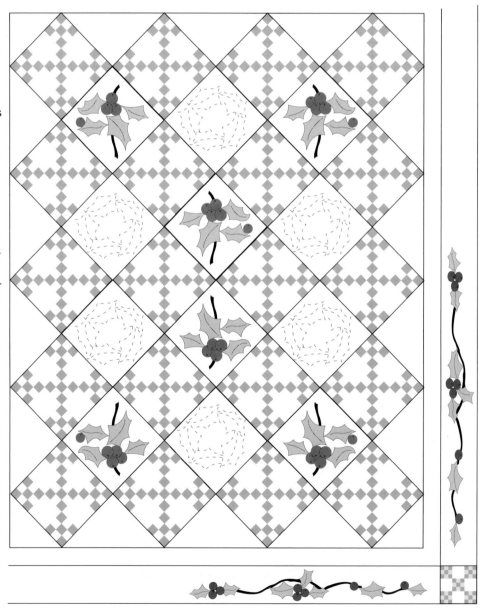

1½"

Red	Green	Red
Green	Red	Green
Red	Green	Red

Muslin

Chain stitch
embroidery after
appliqué.

QUILTING FOR
ALTERNATE BLOCK

Artichoke Frittatas

- 4 eggs, beaten
- 1 small onion, chopped
- 12 salted soda crackers, gently crumbled
- 2 6-ounce jars of marinated artichoke hearts, drained and chopped
- ½ pound of sharp cheddar cheese, finely shredded

Preferred seasonings: tablespoon of Dijon mustard or tablespoon
of chopped fresh savory or oregano, etc.

Mix all ingredients well and bake in an oiled 9" × 9" pan at 350° for 30 to 40 minutes. Cool thoroughly. Cut into squares and reheat before serving. This freezes well, for relatively short periods of time. Thaw to room temperature, then reheat.

Claire Jarratt: Partridge in a Pear Tree

Color picture on page 57

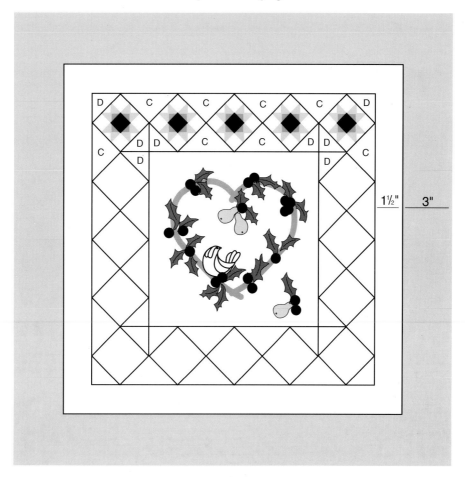

YARDAGE

The finished size of the quilt is 36" square.

- 1 yard of muslin (background and C triangles)
- ¾ yard (outer border, berries, and binding)
- ¼ yard (inner border)
- ¼ yard (leaves and stem)
- 6 or 7 pieces ⅛ yard each for stars and bird, or assorted scraps
- 1¼ yards for backing
- 40" × 40" of batting
- Matching threads for appliqués
- Sulky® gold metallic thread for quilting
- All fabrics should be pre-washed.

CUTTING

- Cut outer border fabric, 4 strips 3½" × 44".
- Cut inner border fabric, 4 strips 2" × 44".
- Cut background square 16¾" × 16¾".
- Cut 64 A star background squares.
- Cut 16 A star centers.
- Cut 64 B background triangles.
- Cut 64 B red print triangles.
- Cut 128 B green print triangles.
- Cut 16 C background triangles.
- Cut 8 C solid-color triangles.
- Cut 4 D background triangles.
- Cut 12 D solid-color triangles.
- Cut four strips 1" × 44" for binding.

Appliqués: Cut the appropriate number of each shape: cut as given for machine appliqué, add ¼" seam allowance for hand appliqué. Stems are ¼" wide. Using a heart outline, be creative with the number and placement of holly, berries, leaves, stems, pears, and partridge.

ASSEMBLY

1. Following the diagram for assembly of pieces, make 16 Ohio Stars. First make the four pieced small squares from the quarter-square triangles. Assemble them with the plain squares into three horizontal rows, then sew the rows together to complete the star.

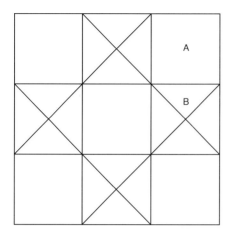

2. Appliqué your chosen arrangement in the basic heart shape.

3. Sew the Ohio Star border, assembling it as shown.

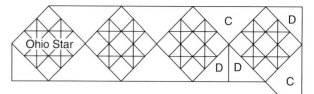

4. Adjust the size of the appliquéd square to fit within the pieced border, and sew them together. First sew the border strips to the appliquéd square, then join the border pieces by the C triangles that interlock the four strips.

4. Attach the inner border to the outer border.

5. Attach these two borders to the quilt, mitering the corners.

6. Layer the top, batting, and backing.

7. Quilt with the gold thread. Be inventive! Mine has the following quilting: cable in the outer border; ⅜" in from each edge of the inner border; around the center square of each star, and in the ditch around the block; crosshatch about ⅝" apart behind all of the appliqué; in the ditch around all appliqués.

8. Attach a binding, in your preferred method. Mine is ¼" wide.

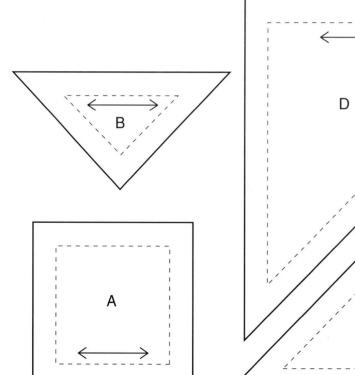

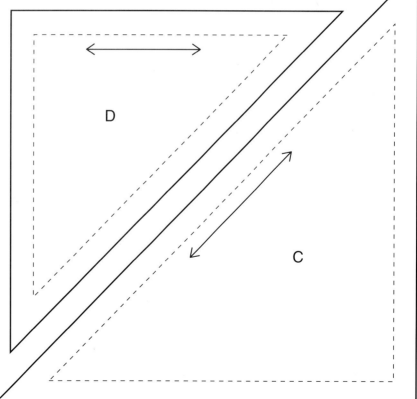

Karen Kinney Drellich: Christmas Cards

Color picture on page 58

Karen Drellich has been my friend for more years than I care to remember, and her late husband was my physician. She was influential in my sending my angel to the Smithsonian, and she came to Washington to help me decorate my tree; she is also on hand in the wee hours to help me edit the directions for my angel kits. Karen has written several books and feature articles, and she teaches extensively. She is particularly known for her inventiveness with a sewing machine, and her clever cards and notes are always a treat to receive.

I began all of these cards with either colored construction paper or Strathmore Blank Greeting Cards, available at art supply stores, 10 cards to a package with envelopes included. The writing and drawing were done with Pilot® gold and silver marking pens and with Tombo Dual Brush-Pens.

I used the decorative stitches on my sewing machines: on some, I put decorative thread in just the bobbin; on others, I put decorative thread through the needle as well. Whenever I used the heavier decorative thread, I used the tension bypass on the bobbin (Elna™), a black latch bobbin (Bernina®), or a second bobbin case (New Home® and others). You need a second bobbin case to release tension on the bobbin and to allow the decorative thread to flow freely from the bobbin. It is best to use at least a #10 or #12 needle. Avoid threads, yarns, or ribbons which are too heavy in the bobbin. If the stitch is complicated (for example, the plain green example), use the simplest thread. Always sew slowly, so the thread will not get tangled and create an unwanted knot. If your machine has a slow setting, use it!

It is also fun to create text and graphics on a computer, then sew the cards closed: this works especially well for party invitations, which you can fill with confetti before you stitch them shut.

PEACE

Candlelight™ yarn from YLI ; red knitting tape from Aardvark Adventures; stitched on Bernina 1230, stitch F 20.

JOY

Metallic 601™ thread from YLI ; stitched on Bernina 1230, stitch 18, foot 1.

CHRISTMAS PRESENT

Metallic 601 thread from YLI; variegated blue from Aardvark Adventures; decorative stitch with New Home Memory Craft 7000, set on the widest stitch.

SEASONS

Red and green variegated metallic thread from YLI; triple zigzag or serpentine stitch on Bernina 1230, Stitch 3 with blacklatch bobbin.

This is also a built-in stitch on Elna, New Home, and most zigzag machines; use the tension bypass on Elna, the extra bobbin case for other machines.

PLAIN RED

Folded paper; metallic thread from YLI; Bernina 1230, stitch 16 (feather) or Elna disc 207.

TREE

Mylar® Ribbon Thread™; simple zigzag stitch with the thread through the blacklatch bobbin on the Bernina 1230 or the tension bypass on the Elna.

PLAIN GREEN

Metallic 601 thread from YLI; stitched on New Home Memory Craft 7000.

Nana's Raw Apple Cake

Stir together in a bowl
- 4 cups of raw apples, peeled and sliced thin
- 2 eggs
- 2 cups of sugar
- ½ cup of salad oil

Mix in
- 2 cups of flour
- 2 tsp. cinnamon
- 2 tsp. baking soda
- 1 tsp. salt
- 2 cups of chopped walnuts

Bake in a 9" x 13" pan at 350° for 45 minutes, or until cake tests done. Serve warm with ice cream on top.

Jean Wells: Layered Appliqué Collage

Color picture on page 59

Old laces, linens, buttons, and ribbons have always held a special fascination for me: I am intrigued by their timelessness. I think of my own grandmothers, of their stitching and lace-making. Then I wonder how these embellishments were originally used. By including them in my own clothing and quilting, I keep tradition alive. I especially enjoy tying these fragments of the past together in a collage with "doodle quilting" in a contrasting thread.

The special old laces and linens, old quilts and Santas, add a nostalgic look to my home Christmas decorations. The red scrappy star quilt that no one else in the family wanted is our tree skirt; someday it will belong to my son.

The garments I have made for this book fit right in with my nostalgic Christmas at home. I have been incorporating laces and linens into my clothing designs for several years now, for an updated Victorian look. A collage is created with the ribbons and buttons to enhance the laces and linens. And each piece becomes unique: you won't find exact duplicates of the pieces I have used, but you will be able to find your own treasures.

These projects are an adult blouse and a size 4 child's dress. Begin with simple commercial patterns that have simple fronts, or decorate a collar. In choosing linens to layer, don't lose sight of the scale of the finished project. On my blouse, the center is the corner of a tablecloth; on the dress bodice, it is a napkin. For a child's piece, corners of doilies and collars are the right sizes. As you see on the dress bodice, flat laces make good filler materials. You may also find new linens and laces that will work well. In figure 1, you see the pieces that I used.

Some of the buttons are old, and some are new. I look for buttons of different sizes and shapes, from ¼" to ⅞". The backs of old pearl buttons are rough and discolored: I show these "wrong" sides, to create texture. A purchased charm here and there adds a nice touch. The ribbons and gold trim are also new.

SUPPLY LISTS

Child's Dress (refer to figure 1a for placement of laces and linens)

- Commercial dress pattern, with required yardage and notions
- Linens as indicated in figure 1a
- 3 small ribbon roses
- 2 medium ribbon roses

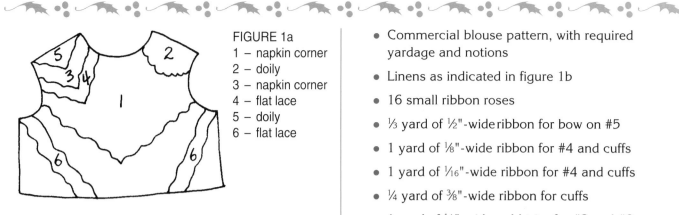

FIGURE 1a
1 – napkin corner
2 – doily
3 – napkin corner
4 – flat lace
5 – doily
6 – flat lace

- ½ yard of cording for #3
- ½ yard of ⅛" ribbon for #2
- ½ yard of ¹⁄₁₆" ribbon for #2
- ⅓ yard of ¼"-wide flat lace for #4
- ⅓ yard of ¼"-wide gold trim (to embellish #4)
- ⅓ yard of 1"-wide flat lace for #6
- 36 buttons
- 2 charms
- Thread to match the trims
- Contrasting thread for doodle quilting
- Monofilament thread for stitching down the linens (optional)

Adult Blouse (refer to figure 1b for placement of laces and linens)

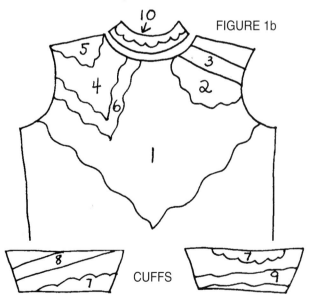

FIGURE 1b

CUFFS

1 – tablecloth corner
2 – doily
3 – flat lace
4 – napkin corner
5 – doily
6 – flat lace
7 – edge of tablecloth
8 – flat lace
9 – flat lace
10 – flat lace

- Commercial blouse pattern, with required yardage and notions
- Linens as indicated in figure 1b
- 16 small ribbon roses
- ⅓ yard of ½"-wide ribbon for bow on #5
- 1 yard of ⅛"-wide ribbon for #4 and cuffs
- 1 yard of ¹⁄₁₆"-wide ribbon for #4 and cuffs
- ¼ yard of ⅜"-wide ribbon for cuffs
- 1 yard of ¼"-wide gold trim for #2 and #8
- ½ yard of ¾"-wide gold trim for #9
- ¼ yard of 1"-wide flat lace for #3
- ⅓ yard of ½"-wide flat lace for #6
- ¼ yard of 1"-wide flat lace for #8
- ¼ yard of 2"-wide flat lace for #9
- ½ yard of 1½"-wide flat lace for #10
- ¼ yard of each of three narrow ribbons for weaving through openings of #3
- 39 buttons
- 3 charms
- Thread to match the trims
- Contrasting thread for doodle quilting
- Monofilament thread for stitching down the linens (optional)

INSTRUCTIONS

Garments

The steps are the same for either the blouse or the dress bodice.

1. Cut out the bodice. On the blouse, determine how far down you want the design to come.

2. Attach the linens and laces in the sequence numbered on figure 1. Pin them in place, and either hand stitch them down or use a sewing machine with monofilament thread in the top.

Embellishments

All of the ribbons and buttons are stitched down by hand, so match the thread to the individual item. Study the photograph to see where the embellishments are placed. Then apply the following specific instructions.

Ribbon Looping

Pin two of the narrower ribbons where you want to start. Make a twist, push the ribbons to stand up, and pin again. See figure 2. Where you have pinned the ribbons to the garment, tack them down. You can then add a ribbon rose or a button over the tacked point.

Bow

Form a bow with your fingers and tack it in the middle. In #5 on my blouse, I added a rose and a charm at the center.

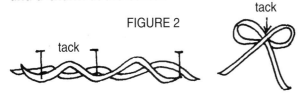

FIGURE 2

Buttons

Stitch all buttons with double thread. Go through the holes twice and knot the thread on the back. Some of the buttons are stitched on top of the ribbon loops; others are stitched around the edge of the doily on #2. The other buttons are clustered. To stitch the button clusters, start by sewing down one button. Position the second button with the holes abutting the edge of the first button, so the second will overlap the first. Overlap three or four buttons for a cluster, then insert ribbon roses and charms.

Doodle Quilting

I use a short running stitch in contrasting thread to fill in some of the empty spaces of the collage. The first row of stitching follows the design along the edges of the linens. Start to meander with the second row, as shown in figure 3. Doodle as you would on paper; it becomes easier with practice.

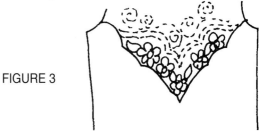

FIGURE 3

Once all of the embellishment is completed, finish sewing the rest of the garment together, as instructed with the pattern.

Grandma's Poppy Seed Cake

- 1 box of yellow cake mix (1 pound, 2½ ounces)
- 1 package of instant vanilla pudding mix (3¾ ounces)
- 4 eggs
- 1 cup of sour cream
- ½ cup of vegetable oil
- ½ cup of cream sherry
- ¼ cup of poppy seeds

Combine all ingredients in a large mixing bowl and stir to blend. Beat at medium speed for 5 minutes. Pour into a 10" greased Bundt pan and bake at 350° for 45 minutes, or until a toothpick comes out clean. Cool on a rack for 15 minutes. Loosen the edges with a knife and turn out onto a plate.

Make a glaze of 1 cup of powdered sugar and 2 to 3 tablespoons of lemon juice. Pour the glaze over the warm cake.

Marinda Stewart: Father Christmas

Color picture on page 61

The first time I ever saw Marinda Stewart, I actually followed her into an elevator to get a closer look at her dress, and I was determined to get to know her; that was over ten years ago. Marinda is one of the most talented women I have ever known: she designs one-of-a-kind garments, has her own pattern company, writes articles for numerous publications, teaches, lectures, and designs for the Fairfield Fashion Show. When I design projects, I make many mistakes: Marinda taught me that there are no mistakes, only re-designing. She was one force prodding me to send my angel to the Smithsonian. For several years I have tried to persuade her to make a Father Christmas, as I knew she would create the ultimate one. (This time, I got to do the prodding.) It is with great pride that I present her creation in this book.

GENERAL TOOLS REQUIRED

- Sewing machine and appropriate thread
- Hot glue gun and glue sticks
- Fabric glue or designer glue (such as Aleene's™ Tacky Glue)
- Fine paint brush
- Doll-making needle (optional, but desirable)
- Clothespins
- Disappearing-ink pen
- Serger (optional)

GENERAL PROCEDURE

1. All seam allowances are ¼".
2. Make and stuff the doll body. Make the head, shape and paint it, and make the hair. Set the head aside.
3. Dress the doll, in this order: shirt; pants; boots and trim; vest, buttons, and watch chain; coat.
4. Put the doll on the stand. Glue the feet in place with hot glue.

5. Glue the toy sack in the doll's right hand. For added stability, you may also wish to glue the sack to the back of the coat. A book may be placed in the crook of the arm.
6. Add the basket to the left arm. Glue the staff in the left hand.
7. Glue the head and hat on the doll.
8. Look the doll over and add final touches to empty areas — pine cones, greens, etc.
9. Glue rings on fingers.
10. Enjoy all your hard play!!

MISCELLANEOUS SUPPLIES

- Small basket
- Doll stand
- Assorted miniature fruit
- 3" wreath
- Wooden staff 12"-14"
- Decorative branches, holly, miniature pine cones
- Small jewels for finger rings

- Appropriate assorted decorations (toys, presents, musical instruments, etc.)

BODY

- ⅜ yards of muslin
- ¼ yard of black fabric for legs, cut crossgrain
- 1 yard of Ewe and Me® white wool roving
- Fabric paint: blue, white, black, red
- Polyester stuffing
- Brown (or black) fine-point permanent marking pen

Legs

1. Right sides together, sew around the edges of the pieces, leaving the end open. Clip the curves. Turn.

2. Stuff each leg firmly to within 1" of the opening, seam to seam with toes forward.

Arms

1. Right sides together, sew around the edges of the pieces, leaving the end open. Clip the curves. Turn.

2. Stuff only the hand, lightly. Top-stitch the fingers as indicated.

3. Finish stuffing the arms firmly, to within 1" of the opening.

Body

1. Pin the arms to the back as indicated, right sides together. The arms should face inward at this point.

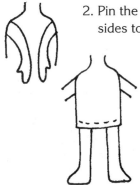

2. Pin the front to the back, right sides together, covering the arms.

3. Sew the side seams from the neck to the hip, leaving the neck and bottom open. Clip the curves. Turn.

4. Turn the seam allowance under at the hip. Attach the legs as

shown, pleating in the fullness of the front as indicated. Top-stitch in place.

5. Firmly stuff the body through the neck opening.

6. Whip stitch the neck closed.

Head

1. Sew the head fronts (edges without notches) right sides together. Clip the curves.

2. Matching the notches, right sides together, sew the head back to front. Clip the curves. Turn.

3. Transfer the face markings with the disappearing-ink pen.

4. Stuff the head firmly.

5. Paint the features as illustrated. Trace the outlines with the fine-tip pen. Paint the eyes and mouth. Draw in wrinkles and eyebrows. Let dry.

6. To shape the face, thread the needle with a double length of thread in a flesh color and knot the end. From inside the head, exit at B for the nose and anchor with a tiny back stitch. Draw the thread along the outside edge of the nose and enter at A. Anchor. Run the thread under the fabric to the same place on the other side of the seam. Pull the thread slightly taut. Exit at A and anchor. Run the thread down the outside of the nose to B and repeat. Do the same for the dots at the base of the nose, making the final exit at the central dot. This will add gentle shaping to the face. Use the same procedure between the inside corners of the eyes to add dimension.

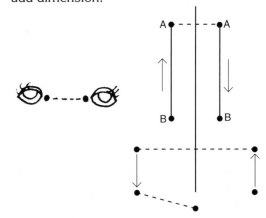

MOUSTACHE

1. Pull a small amount of roving (2"-2½") and fold it in half.

2. Attach it at the fold with a threaded needle at the dot under the nose. Curl the roving around your fingers to shape it.

BEARD

1. Cut two 7" lengths of roving. Fold them in half and gently spread them apart at the folds.

2. Starting at the center of the face, open the roving and back stitch it onto one side of the face along the fold line, using the pattern placement guide. Repeat on the other side. Fold down the top half of the opened roving over the bottom of the beard, concealing the stitches in the fold.

3. Gently blend the two layers of roving together. Arrange the beard. To finish the edge, very gently pluck small amounts of roving from the bottom of the beard to create a naturally irregular edge.

HAIR

1. Fold the remaining roving in half. Gently spread it apart at the fold, as for the beard.

2. Back stitch the hair onto the head, starting at the placement guide on the pattern and continuing for approximately 2½". Create a center part with the back stitches.

3. Pull the hair around to cover the back of the head. Hot glue it in place at the back and sides. Set the head aside until the rest of the doll is dressed, then proceed with the remaining instructions.

4. After the doll has been dressed, make a small cavity in the head stuffing, large enough to accommodate the neck. Put some hot glue in this cavity and glue the head to the doll neck.

5. Finish arranging the hair, beard, and moustache. Pluck the edges of the hair, as you did with the beard, for a natural look. When the hair has been properly arranged, lightly spray it with hair spray.

6. Hot glue the velvet hat to the doll head. Add any additional decorations to the hat.

Shirt

- ⅜ yards of fabric
- 4 small buttons
- ¾ yards of ⅜" ribbon

The shirt may be assembled on a serger.

1. Sew the shirt fronts to the back at the shoulders, right sides together.

2. Fold the facing on the shirt fronts to the inside.

3. Fold the collar in half lengthwise, right sides together. Stitch the ends. Clip the corners. Turn.

4. Sew the collar to the shirt, right sides together. Line up the edges of the collar with the fronts of the shirt. Ease in any fullness.

5. To conceal the raw edges, turn the seams into the neckline. Top-stitch in place.

6. Fold the cuffs in half lengthwise. Gather the cuff edge of the sleeves as indicated. Sew the gathered edge to the cuff through all thicknesses, right sides together.

7. Gather the crown of the sleeve as indicated and sew to the shirt between the dots. Space the gathers evenly. Use the notch on the sleeve to match the shoulder seam.

8. Right sides together and matching the seams and edges, sew the shirt side and sleeve seam in one continuous seam. Back stitch at the cuff edge to anchor it. Turn to the right side.

9. Put the shirt on the doll. Overlap the left side on the top ("male" direction). Sew the buttons on the shirt as indicated through all thicknesses to close.

10. With ribbon, make a multi-loop bow and sew it to the collar front. Fold the bow as shown and top-stitch to hold the loops in place. Tack the bow to the neckline.

Hat and Pants

- ⅜ yards of dark green velveteen
- ½ yard of ¼" elastic
- ⅜ yards of gold trim for hat
- 1" × 14" strip of real or fake fur for hat
- Small amount of stuffing

Hat

1. With right sides together, stitch the ends of the hat band. Fold it in half lengthwise, right sides out.

2. Gather the entire outer edge of the hat circle.

3. Right sides together, sew the hat to the band, adjusting the gathers evenly.

4. Glue the strip of fur to the hat band.

5. Trim the hat with gold braid where the fur joins the hat.

6. Stuff the hat lightly.

7. Glue the hat in place on the head. Add greens.

Pants

1. Join the center seams, right sides together.

2. Fold over the casing at the waist and legs. Stitch in place. Leave a small opening at the waist for inserting elastic.

3. Thread the waistline with the elastic and stitch the overlapped ends of the elastic. Stitch the opening closed.

4. For the legs, thread the casings with elastic. Top-stitch the elastic, in the seam allowance, at each side of each leg to anchor it.

5. Right sides together, stitch the pant legs from one side to the other.

6. Put the pants on the doll. Tuck in the shirt hem.

Boots

- Black lace-up boots for a 19"-24" doll
- 2 pieces of black real or fake fur, 1" × 5" each

Glue a strip of fur to the top of each boot after the boots are put on the doll.

Vest

- ¼ yard of brown velveteen
- ¼ yard of cotton lining
- 3 buttons
- Optional: 6"-8" chain for watch, decorative gold drop for watch fob

1. Cut out the fabric, lining, and welts. Fold the welts in half lengthwise, right sides together.

2. Sew a ¼" seam at each end. Clip the corners. Turn.

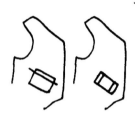

3. Sew the welt onto the vest, using the placement guide. Top-stitch ¼" from the raw edge. Turn the welt up. Top-stitch each end in place. The welt will be sewn on three sides; the raw edges will be out of sight.

4. Right sides together, stitch the lining to the fabric. Leave all shoulder seams open! Clip all curves and corners. Turn through an open shoulder seam.

5. Slide the back shoulder seam into the front shoulder seam. Turn under the ¼" seam allowance. Hand or machine stitch in place, enclosing all raw edges. Repeat for the other shoulder.

6. Put the vest on the doll. Overlap the left side on the top. Stitch three buttons in place through all thicknesses of the fabric to close.

7. Attach the watch chain as indicated.

Coat

- ¾ yards of fabric
- ¾ yards of lining
- 2½ yards of trim (same gold trim as hat, or not, as preferred)
- ⅛ yards of fur, fake fur, or fur fabric

1. Fold the facing of the pocket to the inside. Top-stitch in place.

2. Press under the pocket seam allowance. Pin the pocket to the coat front as indicated. Top-stitch in place.

3. Join the fronts to the back, at the shoulders, right sides together. Repeat for the lining.

4. Sew the sleeves to the coat. Align the markings, match the notch to the shoulder seam and the dots at each edge of the sleeve. Repeat for the lining.

5. With right sides together, sew the underarm seams and the side seams. Press the seams open. Repeat for the lining.

6. Right sides together, pin the lining to the coat around the entire neck edge, down the front, and the bottom hem. Stitch, leaving a small opening on the back hemline for turning the coat to the right side. Clip any curves and turn. Slip-stitch the opening closed.

7. Turn under the seam allowances on the sleeves and lining, and slip-stitch together.

8. Cut 1" strips of fur and, with designer or fabric glue, attach the fur around the outer edges of the coat and sleeves.

9. Glue trim in place along the edge where the fur joins the coat.

10. When all glue is dry, put the coat on the doll.

Toy Sack

- ¼ yard of fabric
- 1 yard of cording

- Polyester stuffing or crumpled newspaper to stuff the bottom (paper gives a more authentic look, since it creates bulges, as if of other toys)

- Assorted toys, packages, branches, balls, books, etc.

1. Sew the seams, right sides together. Turn.

2. Turn under the casing and stitch. Leave an opening for the cord.

3. Thread the cord through the casing. Knot the ends. (optional) Add small bells or ornaments to the ends of the cords.

4. Stuff the sack ¾ full with polyester or newspaper. (See note above.)

5. Put the toys and other objects into the sack, and hot glue them in place.

6. Pull the sack partially closed. Glue into the doll's right hand. Secure temporarily with a clothespin until the glue dries.

Staff

Add the staff and the toy sack only after the doll is completely dressed and set into the stand.

1. Decorate the top of the staff as desired.

2. Position it in the doll's left hand, after the small basket has been hung on the left arm. Make sure the bottom of the staff touches the ground.

Chocolate Walnut Cookies

I usually bake cookies as gifts for friends, packaging them in reusable gift containers. If I go into San Francisco on Christmas day, I make a package of three or four cookies and give it to the toll collector on the Bay Bridge, who has to work on this family holiday. The reactions are priceless!

Cream ¼ cup of butter with ¼ cup of shortening. Add ¾ cup of sugar gradually and beat well. Beat in one egg. Stir in two 1-ounce squares of melted, unsweetened chocolate. Add 1¾ cups of flour sifted with ½ teaspoon of baking soda and ½ teaspoon of salt. Alternate with ½ cup of milk. Mix well. Stir in 1 teaspoon of vanilla extract and ½ cup of chopped walnuts. Drop the dough by teaspoonfuls onto an ungreased cookie sheet, leaving 2" between drops. Bake at 400° for 8 to 10 minutes. Cool on a rack. This recipe yields approximately 3 dozen cookies.

To frost, add enough milk or cream to 2 cups of sifted powdered sugar, to make a frosting that spreads easily. Add a dash of salt and 1 teaspoon of vanilla extract. Frost the tops of the cookies and garnish each with a walnut half.

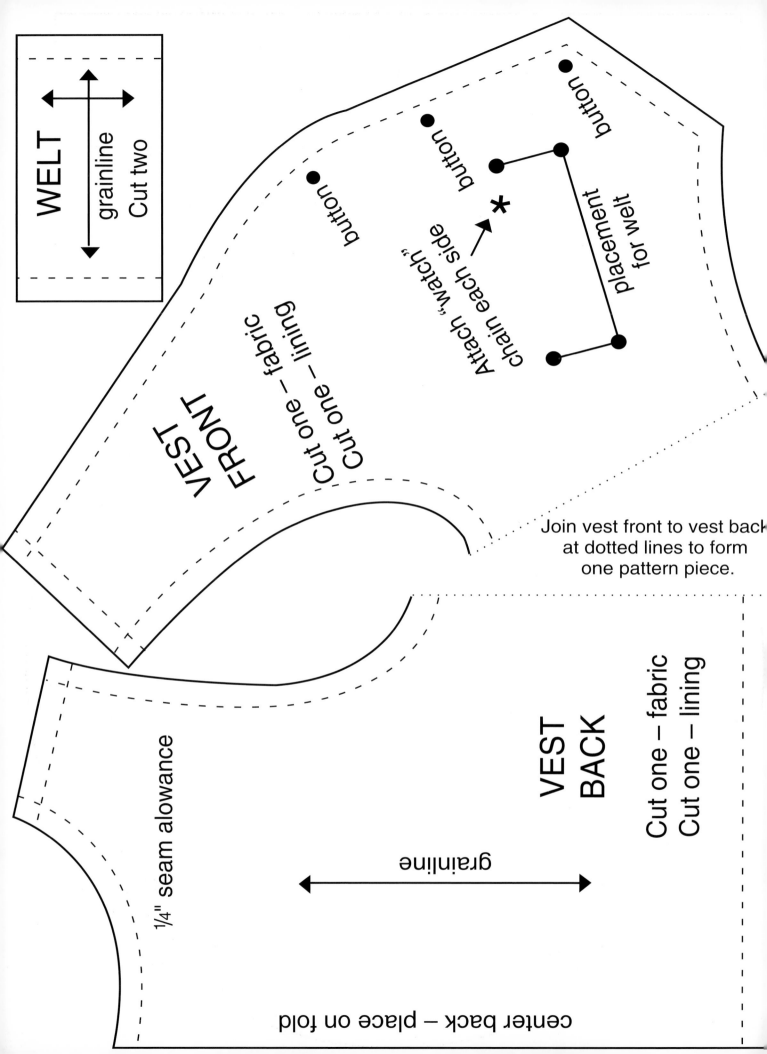

WELT

grainline

Cut two

VEST FRONT

Cut one – fabric
Cut one – lining

button

button

button

Attach "watch"
chain each side

*

placement
for welt

Join vest front to vest back
at dotted lines to form
one pattern piece.

VEST BACK

Cut one – fabric
Cut one – lining

¼" seam alowance

grainline

center back – place on fold

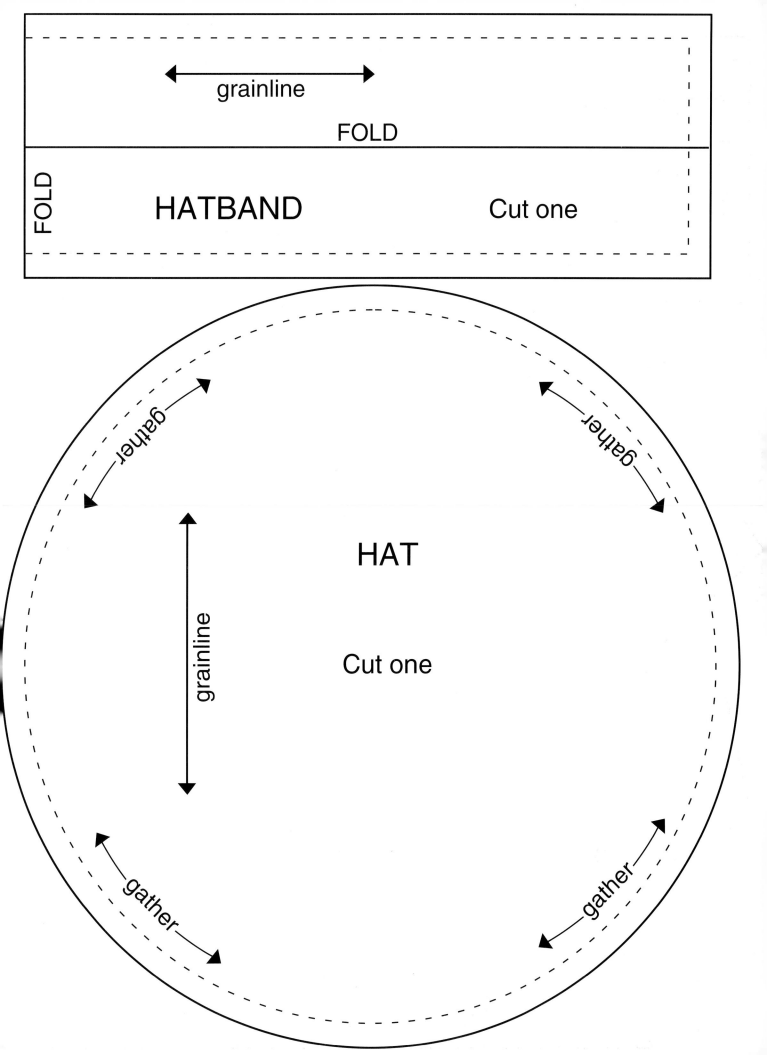

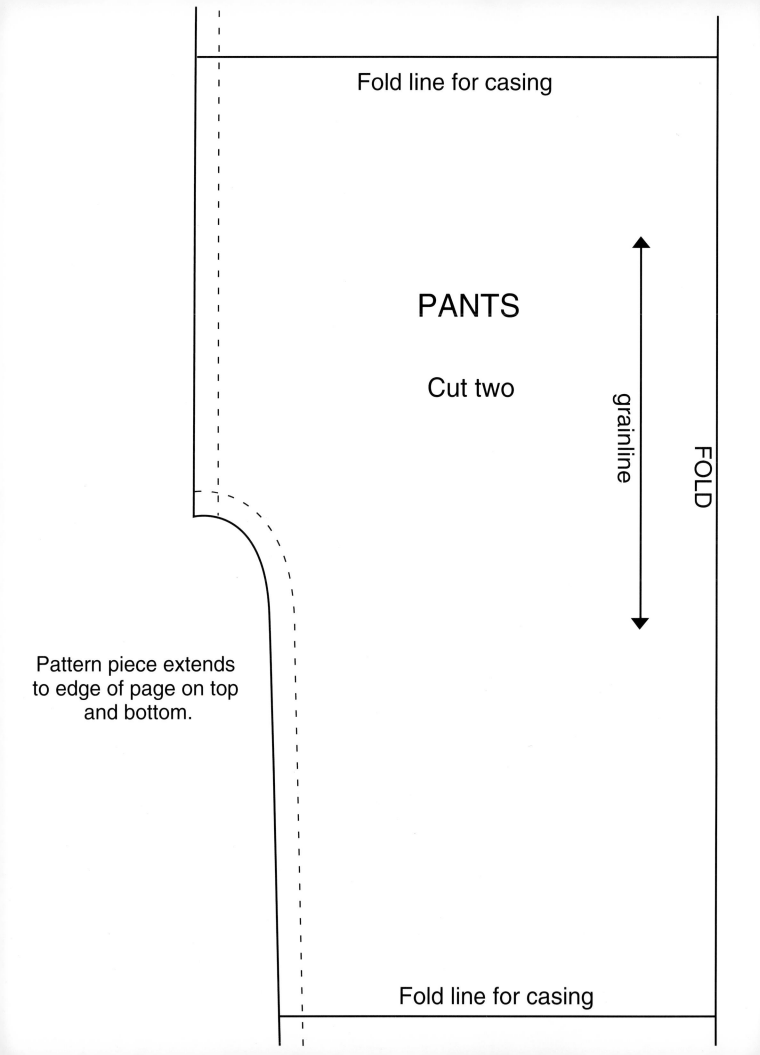

Fold line for casing

PANTS

Cut two

grainline

FOLD

Pattern piece extends
to edge of page on top
and bottom.

Fold line for casing

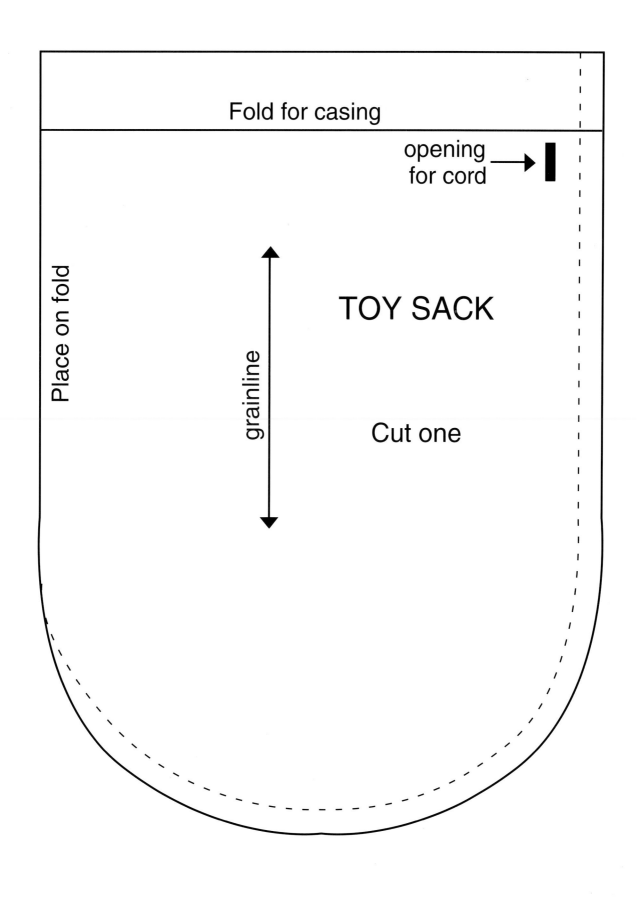

Fold for casing

opening
for cord

Place on fold

TOY SACK

grainline

Cut one

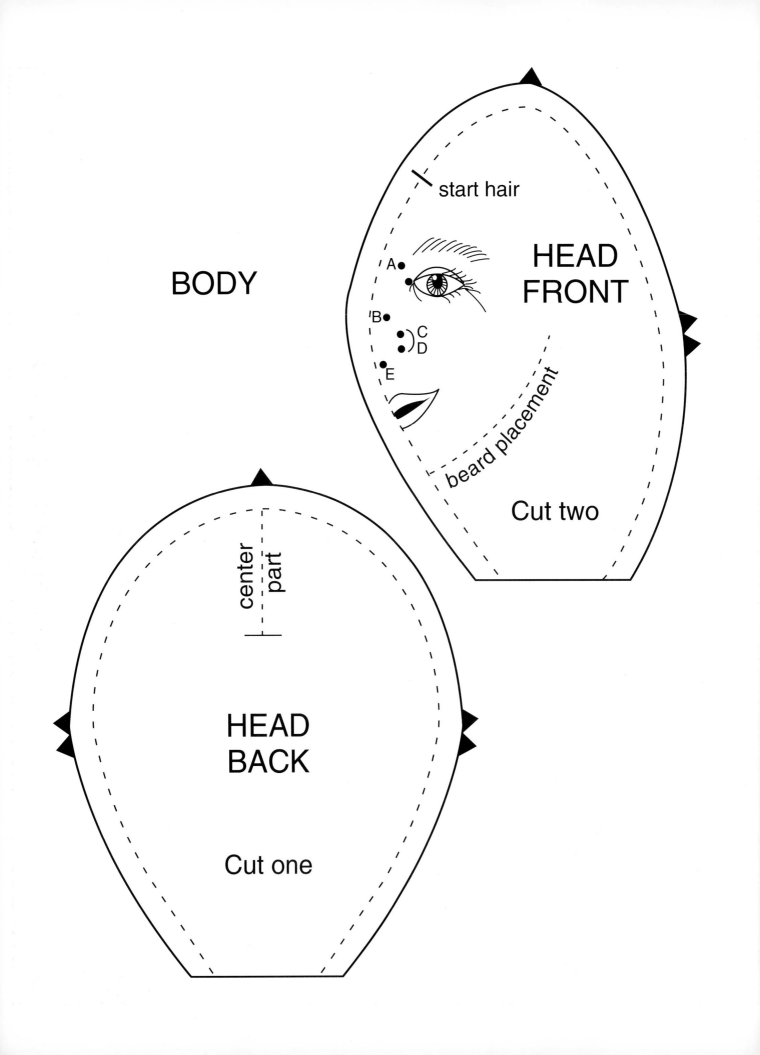

BODY

start hair

A •
B •
C
D
E

HEAD
FRONT

beard placement

Cut two

center part

HEAD
BACK

Cut one

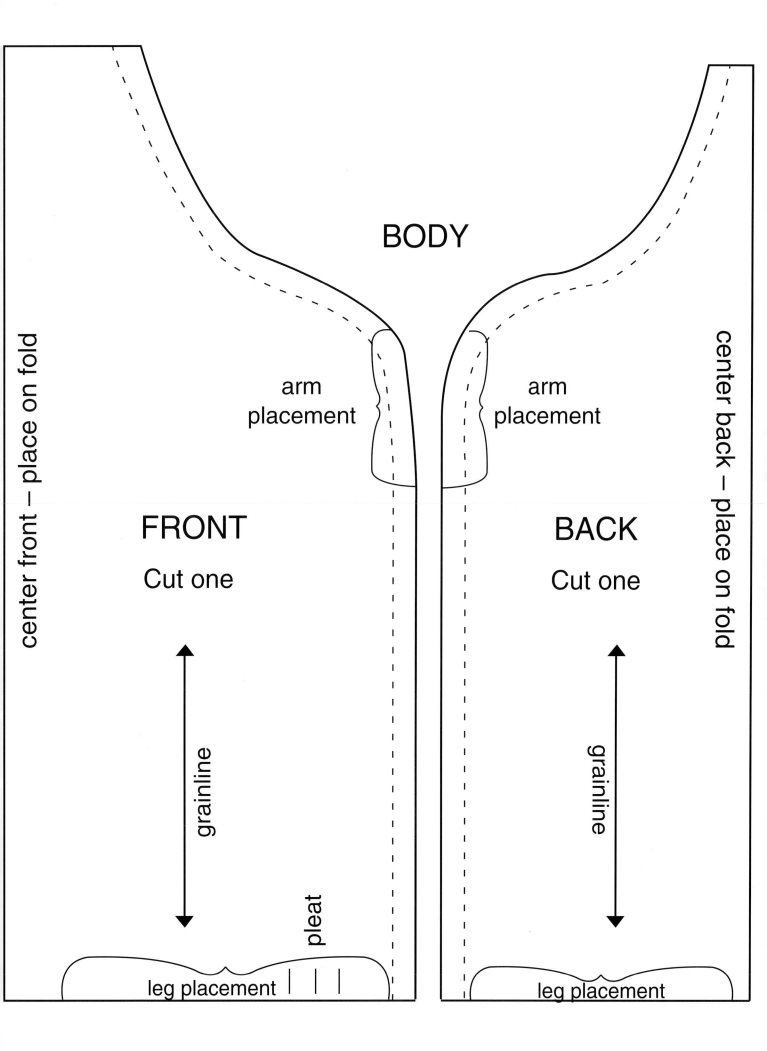

BODY

center front – place on fold

center back – place on fold

arm
placement

arm
placement

FRONT

Cut one

BACK

Cut one

grainline

grainline

pleat

leg placement

leg placement

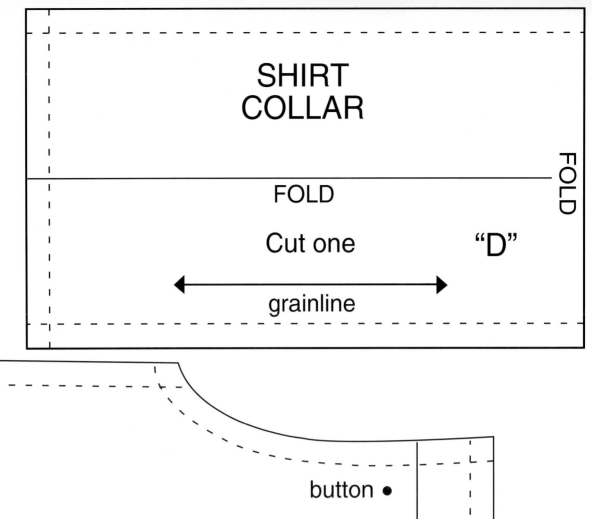

SHIRT COLLAR

FOLD

Cut one   "D"

← grainline →

FOLD

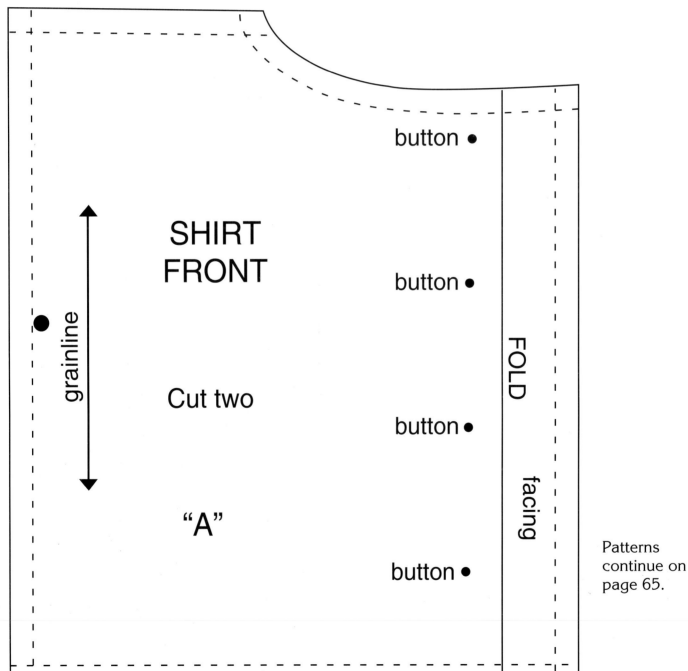

button •

SHIRT FRONT

button •

grainline

Cut two

FOLD

button •

facing

"A"

button •

Patterns continue on page 65.

THE PROJECTS

Margaret Peters:
Bundle of Love

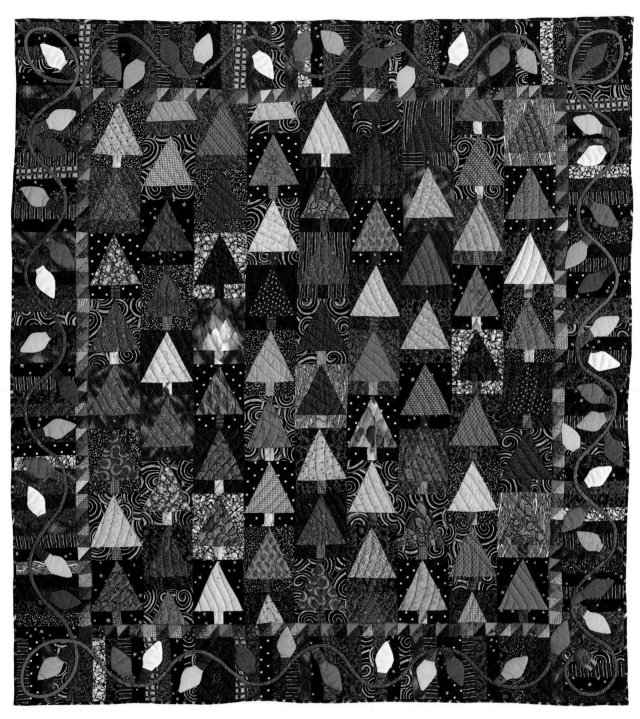

Alex Anderson:
Flying Trees

Sally Collins:
Oh Christmas Tree

Anna Judd Edwards:
Peace on Earth

Rosalee Sanders:
'Twas The Night Before Christmas

 Rhondi Hindman:
Cookie Cutter Quilt

Claire Jarratt:
Double Nine-Patch

Claire Jarratt:
Partridge in a Pear Tree

Karen Kinney Drellich:
Christmas Cards

Jean Wells:
Layered Appliqué Collage

Marinda Stewart:
Father Christmas

Pat Carriker:
Pat C Bear Ornament

Gretchen Jennings:
Santa in His Sleigh

 Miriam Gourley:
Cosette's Doll

Clothing modeled by Elizabeth and Kylie Duthie

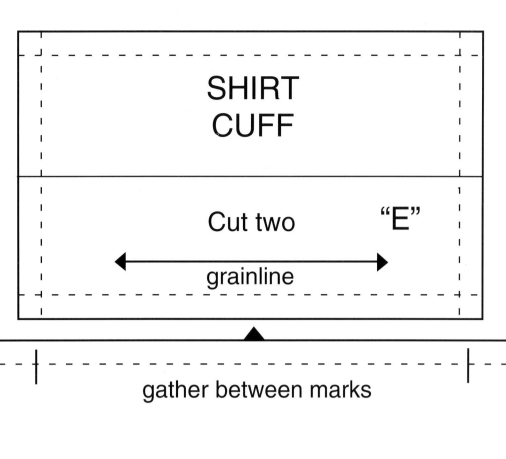

SHIRT
CUFF

Cut two   "E"

grainline

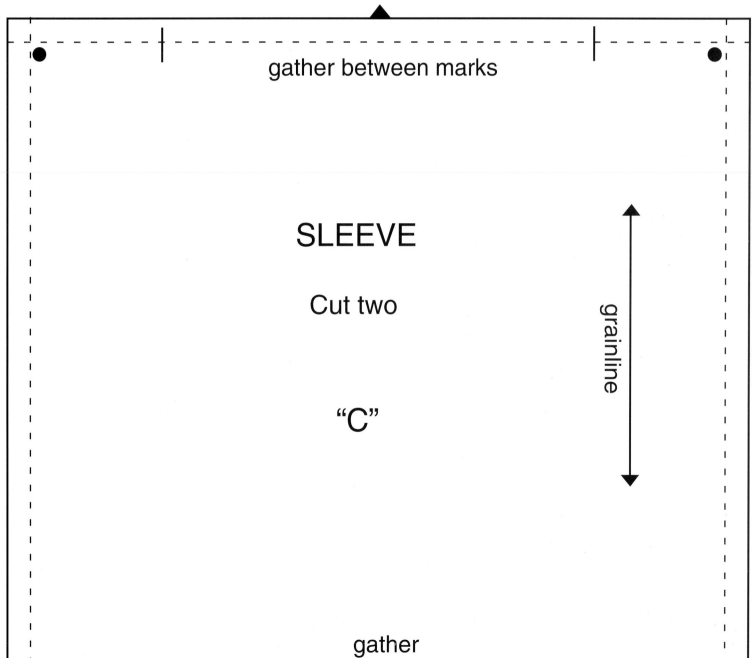

gather between marks

SLEEVE

Cut two

"C"

grainline

gather

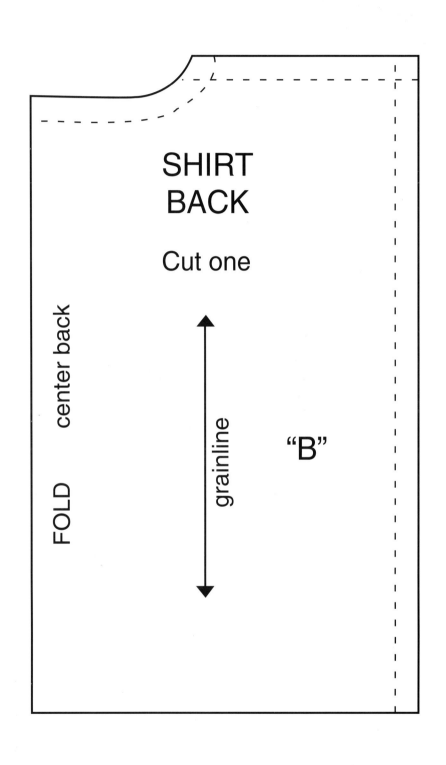

SHIRT
BACK

Cut one

center back

FOLD

grainline

"B"

Additional patterns are inserted at the back of the book.

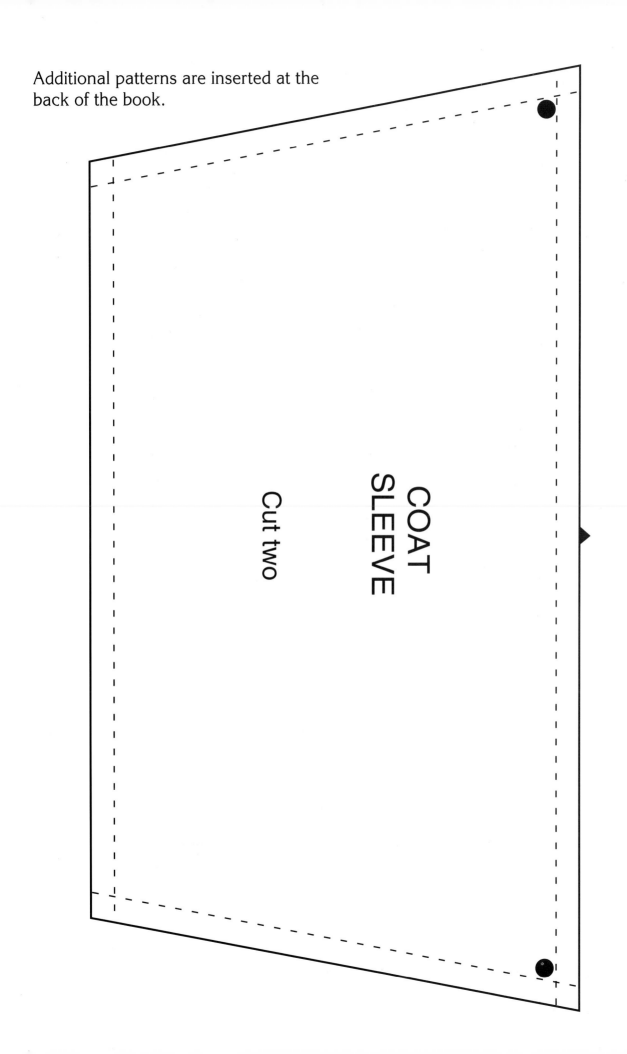

COAT
SLEEVE

Cut two

Pat Carriker: Pat C Bear Ornament

Color picture on page 62

If you collect teddy bears, Pat Carriker's name is already familiar; if not, you are about to receive a rare treat. For Pat to share one of her dear bears is a true honor. I have known Pat for a half-dozen years; in fact, it was for her that I made one of my angels, eventually leading to my making the tree for the Smithsonian Institution. (But that's another story, for another time.) Pat's specialty is tiny bears that depict all phases of life, from Prom Queen to Carpenters to Uncle Sam. She always has a basket in her lap, divided into sections of bear arms, legs, and bodies waiting to be brought to life. The whimsy of the bears reflects Pat and her personality: would that we all had her energy!

SUPPLIES NEEDED

- Cotton stretch velour
- A small piece of contrasting velour for the nose
- Two 2 mm. black beads for the eyes (optional)
- Black embroidery thread
- Calico for dresses
- Unbleached muslin for aprons and backing of heart
- Strong carpet thread
- 4" × 4" Aida cloth (14 count) for counted cross-stitch heart
- Polyfiber stuffing
- Needles — any comfortable ones

BEAR

Trace the pattern to use as a template. Fold the velour, right sides together, and trace the bear pattern onto the wrong side of the fabric. First stitch on the traced lines, then cut out, leaving a ⅛" edge. Clip open as indicated by the dotted lines, through one thickness only. Turn the bear inside out and stuff it with polyfiber, then sew the opening closed with a slip stitch. Thread your needle with carpet thread and tack the neck edge, then wrap the thread several times around the neck to create the neck and shoulders. Pull tight and tack off.

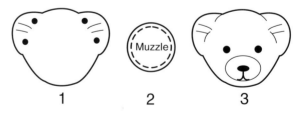

With carpet thread, form the ears by inserting the needle from the top to the bottom of the ear, then pulling the thread to form a cup shape. Tack off. Cut out the muzzle circle. With running stitches ⅛" from the edge, pull slightly to create a small ball, then add a bit of stuffing and tighten a bit more. Slip stitch the muzzle into place on the head. Then sew on beads for the eyes, or make French knots with embroidery thread. Sew the nose and mouth details with black embroidery thread.

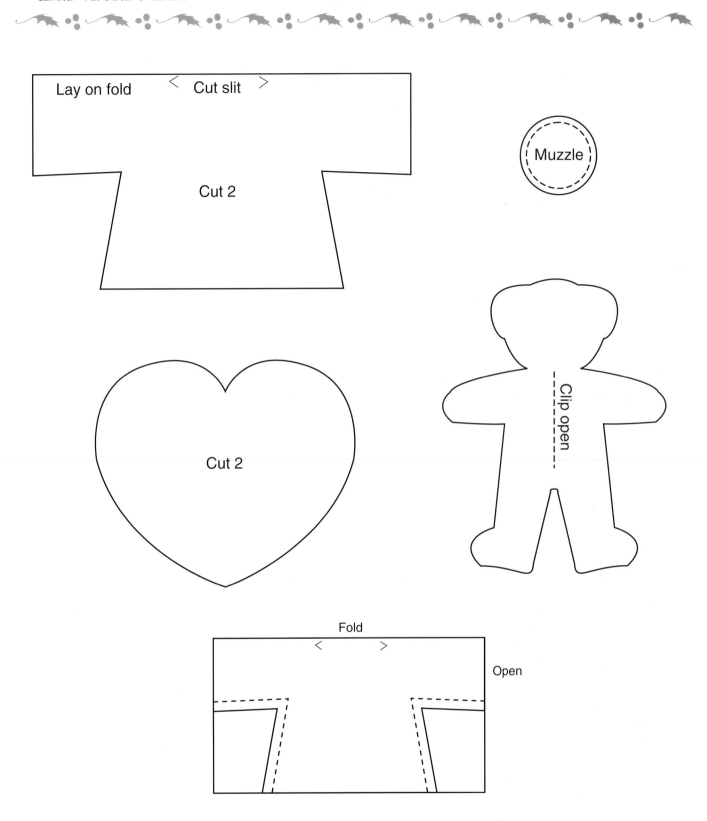

Lay on fold   < Cut slit >

Cut 2

Muzzle

Cut 2

Clip open

Fold
< >

Open

DRESS

Trace the dress pattern onto calico. Sew the pieces together on the dotted line, from under the sleeve on down the side of the dress. Cut out, leaving a ⅛" seam allowance. Slit the neckline open as indicated. Sew a small hem on the bottom. Put the dress on the bear, turn the neck edge under and sew it with a small running stitch, then pull and adjust it to the bear's neck. Tack off. Fit the sleeves in the same way.

APRON

You will need a 3" × 1⅛" piece of unbleached muslin for the apron, and a ⅝" × 6" strip of muslin for the tie band.

Sew a small hem along the sides of the apron. Pull several threads on the bottom edge to make a fringe. Gather the top to measure 1¼". Place the tie band on as pictured, turn the band over and top-stitch it. Put it on the bear, over the dress, and tie it with a knot in the back.

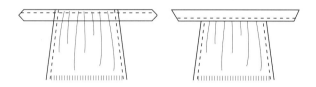

HEART

After working the cross-stitch pattern, lay it face down on a piece of unbleached muslin. Machine stitch around the heart, leaving a small opening on one side. Cut it out and turn it; stuff with polyfiber and close the opening with a slip stitch.

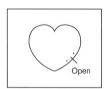
Open

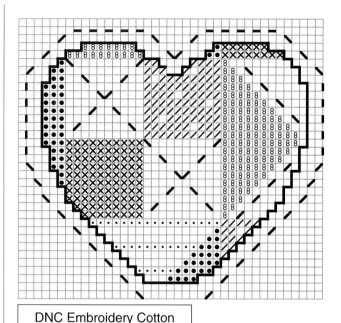

DNC Embroidery Cotton
☐ 500 (back stitch only)
● 520   ╱ 524   • 221
✕ 522   8 814

Ecru–fill in all open spaces if not stitched on white fabric.

Raisin Carrot Cake

Sift together, then set aside
- 2 cups of flour
- 2 teaspoons of baking soda
- 1 teaspoon of salt
- 1 teaspoon of cinnamon

Cover 2 cups of raisins with warm water and let them stand 5 minutes. Then drain and blot them dry with paper towels.
Chop ½ cup of nuts.
Chop 2 cups of apples (about 2 medium).
Coarsely grate 3 cups of carrots (about 5 carrots).

In a large bowl, beat together well
- 2 cups of sugar
- 4 eggs
- 1 cup of vegetable oil

Then mix in the flour mixture. Add the raisins, nuts, apples, and carrots, stirring well. Pour the completed mixture into two loaf pans. Bake at 350° for 45 minutes, or until the cake tests as done.

Gretchen Jennings: Santa in His Sleigh

Color picture on page 62

Three years ago I signed up for a doll-making class in Sacramento from Gretchen Jennings, and a warm and wonderful friendship was born. Gretchen is a delight to know and be with, and she is very dedicated to her students. She sprinkles her teaching with personal family anecdotes, and they enrich the family lives of the students. Her talent knows no bounds, nor does her enthusiasm. Everyone needs a Gretchen Jennings: she is a major star in my book of valued friends.

SUPPLY LIST

- 1 small spool of 20-gauge stainless steel wire
- 2 egg-shaped ⅛-oz. lead fishing weights
- One 1-oz. river sinker lead fishing weight
- Super Sculpey®
- Cream shoe polish, neutral and brown
- Acrylic paints: blue, white, black, terra cotta
- 1 #0 paint brush
- 1 braid of wool roving, white or blond
- Four 1" strips of lightweight quilt batting
- ¼ yard of red wool, velvet, patriotic cottons or scraps for suit and hat
- 3" square knit, fur, or contrast fabric for mittens
- Scraps of kid, thin leather, or Ultrasuede® for boots, belt, and toy bag
- Scraps of real or fake fur for suit trimmings
- Assortment of small toys, key-chain ornaments, gift tie-ons, boxes, etc.
- Tacky glue
- Wooden or metal sleigh
- Needlenose pliers
- Bow whip, skewer, or hemostat
- Tiny bell for Santa's hat
- 1 brown Pigma Micron® permanent pen for face, signing and dating
- ½ cup of aquarium gravel or small stones
- 1 handful of polyester stuffing

SANTA'S BODY

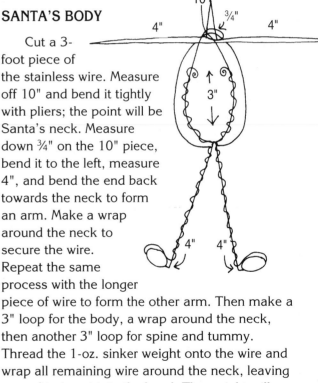

Cut a 3-foot piece of the stainless wire. Measure off 10" and bend it tightly with pliers; the point will be Santa's neck. Measure down ¾" on the 10" piece, bend it to the left, measure 4", and bend the end back towards the neck to form an arm. Make a wrap around the neck to secure the wire. Repeat the same process with the longer piece of wire to form the other arm. Then make a 3" loop for the body, a wrap around the neck, then another 3" loop for spine and tummy. Thread the 1-oz. sinker weight onto the wire and wrap all remaining wire around the neck, leaving an end to insert into the head. The weight will dangle freely until the body is stuffed.

Cut another 2-foot piece of wire and bend it in half for the legs. Thread one ⅛-oz. weight onto one leg and bend the wire 4" from the center, so the weight becomes the foot. Bend the rest of the wire on that half back and twist it up the leg, to reinforce it (you'll have extra wire). Repeat this process for the second foot and leg. Fit this leg unit over the lower loop of the body and twist the extra pieces of wire around body loop wires. Curl the tips of the wires around the pliers, so they will not later push out through the fabric.

SANTA'S HEAD

There are four layers of material in a one-pound box of Super Sculpey, and each layer is divided into 7 strips. Soften one strip and shape it into a ball. Visually divide the ball in half; ¼" from the bottom of the ball, pull a neck downward and smooth it with your thumb. The neck will be about ½" around and a little more than ½" long — and Santa will now resemble ET. Choose a surface for his face. Soften a piece of Super Sculpey the size of a pencil eraser and form it into a log shape. Press it vertically onto the head so that the bottom of the log is ¾ of the way down the face and smooth the top of the log to blend it in. Then blend the sides of the log into the face, so you have shaped a nose. (The eyes and mouth will be painted later.) Gently place the head onto the ¾" neck wires and pinch at the base to secure it.

Bake this in an oven for about 10 minutes at 250°, on a piece of foil or a cookie sheet. Allow it to cool, at which point it should be totally hardened to the fingernail. If it is not hard enough when it is cool, re-bake another 5 to 8 minutes and re-test it.

To paint the face, mark the center of the eye with a pencil dot (just a reference point), vertically midway down the face. With white paint, paint two crescent shapes, points downward. When the white paint has dried, paint a circle to make the irises in your preferred color. When those have dried, add the small black pupils. Also add a fleck of white on the same side of each iris, to make the eyes sparkle. With thinned terra cotta paint, add a brush stroke of blush to each cheek and the tip of the nose. Use unthinned terra cotta for Santa's happy grin. Outline and accentuate the eyes and the dried mouth with the brown pen.

Blend together in a jar a half-teaspoon of neutral polish and a capful of brown polish and smooth the mix over all the Sculpey surfaces with a soft cloth. When the polish has dried, repeat the process. After the second drying, buff lightly.

While waiting for the polish to dry, wrap the body mummy-style with thin quilt batting cut into 1" strips. Cover all wire and weights, tucking the end of the first strip into the tummy to keep the weight in place. To secure the ends of the batting, you can either tuck them into the wraps or tie them with thread.

To make Santa's beard, scrape off a strip of wax from the face, from ear to ear and just below his mouth, as well as under his nose. Squeeze a line of glue onto the beard area. Pull apart both ends of a 2" length of wool braid and lay it in place for the beard. Mash it down into the glue, pulling the strands in the growth direction with a long pin. Measure 1" of braid and separate the strands. Scrape the back of the head, apply glue and add the hair, removing two curls for the moustache and eyebrows. Again mash the hair with a pin. Put a dab of glue under the nose and center one curl of hair for the moustache. Scrape a small line above each eye and trace it with glue. Clip the remaining curl into ⅛" lengths, place and shape the eyebrows.

SANTA'S CLOTHES

Cut pieces of fabric using the pattern pieces: note the folds! All seams are ⅛" and are included on the patterns except for the mittens, which are sewn on the tracing line before cutting, to prevent raveling. Open out both trouser pieces and lay them right sides together, then sew both curved crotch seams. Open to form the trousers, matching heart markings together, then sew from ankle to ankle. Turn the trousers and put them on Santa; slip stitch the raw waist edge to his body, gathering slightly to adjust the fit if necessary.

Lay the right sides of the jacket together and stitch the shoulder seams. Open. Lay the right side of the jacket wrist to the right side of a fur piece which you have cut to fit the sleeve; stitch them together. Repeat for the other sleeve. Open the

jacket flat and, with the right sides together, sew the seam from the wrist to the waist, on both sides. Clip under the arm. Match a fur strip and sew it to the bottom of the jacket. Stitch a fur strip down the left front of the jacket. Turn the jacket and put it on Santa; slip stitch the fur front to the right side of the jacket to close it. You can now add antique buttons, a leather strip for a belt, and a tiny belt buckle purchased in a notions department.

Sew two cap shapes together. With right sides together, attach a fur strip to the cap. Turn, sew a small bell on the tip. With a spot of glue, attach the cap to Santa's head. Stitch the boots with wrong (yes!) sides together, leaving the tops open. Press the foot down flat onto each sole and glue. When the boots are dry, put them on Santa and tuck his trousers into his boots. You can make a band of fur to slip over the boot and glue it to the top. Trace the mitten pattern onto knit fabric, sew on the tracing line, cut out, and turn. Put them on Santa's hands and tack them to the wrists. Sew Santa's toy bag right sides together and turn. Put ½ cup of aquarium gravel or small stones in the bottom of the bag, then add polyester stuffing to just below the dotted line: this is the gathering line for a cord or leather tie, to give his bag shape and to keep the toys in place. Cover the stuffing with glue and arrange the toys on top.

Now put Santa in his sleigh. To bend him, hold the body firmly and bend each knee, then bend the arms to wave or to hold toys. He can also bend forward or back at the waist, but you'll have to be extremely careful if you try to bend his head: very slowly, gripping the base of the neck. Sign the bottom of his boot with your name and the date, since this will surely become a treasured family heirloom.

TOYS

Flags

- Toothpick flags sold for cake decorating

Drums

- 1" of 1" dowel for each drum
- 2 circles of kid or Ultrasuede, 1¼" each

- Button twist, ⅛" ribbon, or embroidery floss
- Acrylic paints
- 2 round toothpicks
- 2 small wooden beads
- Tacky glue
- Brown shoe polish
- Large-eyed needle

Paint all around (but not the ends) each piece of dowel, and decorate with stars, stripes, flags, etc. While the paint is drying, glue one end of each round toothpick into a small bead, then paint the drumsticks to match the drum. Antique the drum by wiping it with brown shoe polish and buffing it. Thread a large-eyed needle with button twist, make a small single-strand knot, then stitch a zigzag of thread to hold leather ends on the drum and make a decorative pattern. Then insert the drumsticks under the laces and glue in place.

Doll

- 6" piece of 20-gauge wire
- Super Sculpey
- Scrap of cotton for dress
- Scrap of braid wool roving (any color)

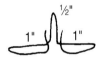 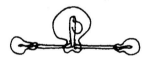

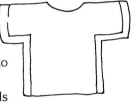

Cut a 6" piece of wire and bend it in half, pinching tightly with pliers. Follow the diagram to make a doll with 1" arms. Pinch all bends and the ends together at a ½" neck. Roll a ball of Super Sculpey the size of a garbanzo bean. Pull out a nose and pull down a neck to cover all wire ends, and stick the head onto the armature. Roll two small peas of Super Sculpey and pinch onto wire for hands. Bake with the head at 250° for 10-15 minutes: the material should not change color, and should be hard when cooled. Trace the dress onto cloth, using the pencil line as your stitching line. Sew, turn, and cut the neck. Turn the sleeves under ⅛", gather by hand, and pull tight around the wrists. Repeat for the neck. Add a tiny bit of stuffing. You do not have to finish the bottom.

Ice Skates

- WonderUnder®
- 2 pieces of 4" × 4" black or white fabric
- Tacky glue
- 2 pieces 2" each of 20-gauge wire
- Button twist or embroidery floss
- 2 pieces 1½" × 1" of sock or thin sweater ribbing
- Large-eyed needle

For stability, bind two pieces of 4" × 4" black or white fabric together with WonderUnder. Trace the pattern onto the fabric. Using the tracing line as your stitching line, stitch between the heart markings. Turn. Glue a tongue inside each skate at the heart mark by the toe. Thread a large-eyed needle with button twist and lace up the skate, leaving the laces loose to tie together so the pair will hang from the toy bag. Bend 2" of wire into a blade shape, as pictured. Stick the end of the wire into the shoe, flatten ½" along the inside of the sole, glue. Repeat for the other shoe. Cut 2 pieces of 1½" × 1" of ribbing. Stitch the long sides of each separate piece to form 2 tubes, each ½" × 1½". Turn. Stuff each into a skate, leaving ½" poking out to resemble socks. Tie the skates together by the laces.

Horse on a Stick

- 4" of ⅛" dowel
- Scrap of leather or checked fabric
- Embroidery floss or button twist
- Strip of leather, Ultrasuede, or ⅛" leather shoelace

- 2 tiny black glass beads
- Small bit of polyester stuffing
- Tacky glue
- Large-eyed needle

Trace the pattern onto scraps of checked fabric or leather. Use the pencil line as the stitching line, leaving the bottom of the neck open. Turn, using a bow whip, a skewer, or a hemostat. Stuff tightly with polyester. Turn the raw edge under ⅛", gather it around a 4" piece of ⅛" dowel, pull tight, and knot. Use the button twist or embroidery floss to make the mane and forelock: thread the needle with single strands, pull through just each side of the back seam behind the ear, pull to about 1", knot on the seam, cut, and continue on down the mane. Make several similar stitches in front of the ear for a forelock. Make a bridle and reins of the leather strip or shoelace.

Santa parties were a regular event in our family, wherever we lived, during the youthful years of our sons, Crist and Jon. We would gather with their friends and their friends' families for an evening dessert, with games and a surprise visit from Santa. He would entertain each child with a few personal stories, a candy cane, and encouragement for good behavior. The year we moved to California from Wisconsin shortly after Christmas, our friends helped to continue the tradition for us while we prepared for the moving van; Santa assured our boys that he had already checked out the chimney in the California house, where he would see them the following year.

As we made the transition from Santa parties to more grown-up gatherings, a favorite dessert entered our annual festivities — a Yule Log taught to me by a fellow teacher in 1965. We have made a 15" log for small parties, up to a 90" log as a grand centerpiece, resting on a bed of evergreens, sprouting meringue mushrooms and dusted with powdered-sugar snow. I make each log individually and roll it in its own cloth, spreading the cream at the last minute; then Bob carries it to the dining room, where it receives the final trimmings.

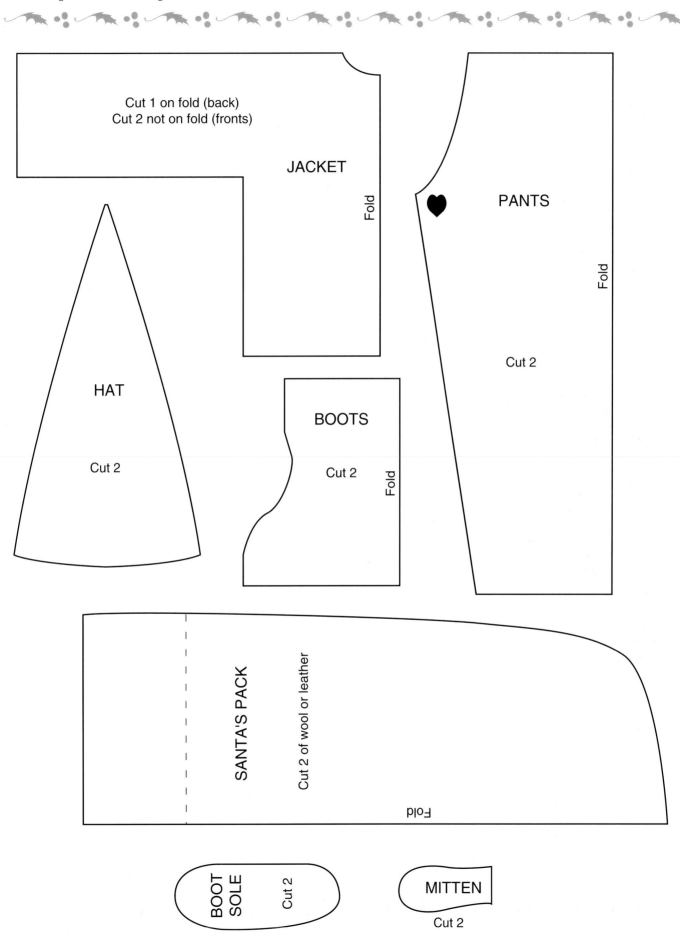

Yule Log

- 5 eggs, separated
- 1 teaspoon of baking powder
- 4 tablespoons of flour
- 3 tablespoons of cocoa
- Dash of salt
- 2 tablespoons of water
- ⅔ cup of powdered sugar

Beat the egg whites and set aside. Add all the dry ingredients except the sugar to the yolks and beat the mixture, adding the water. With the mixer on a slow setting, fold the mixture into the whites. Line a 15½" × 10½" × 1" jelly roll pan with waxed paper, then spread the mixture in the pan. Bake at 325° for 25 minutes. Sift powdered sugar onto a tea towel and tip the hot cake onto the towel, gently removing the waxed paper (gentle prodding with a knife helps). Roll a 15" roll and allow it to cool. If you are making more than one roll, mix the second while the first is baking. When the rolls have cooled, they can be removed from the towels, wrapped in waxed paper, and frozen until needed.

Whipped Cream Filling

- ½ pint of whipping cream
- ½ teaspoon of vanilla extract
- 3 tablespoons of powdered sugar
- ¼ cup of crushed peppermint candies (optional)

Whip the cream to form soft peaks, then add the vanilla and sugar and continue beating (briefly) until the mixture is stiff. Fold in the candies, if desired. Do not fill the cakes until ready to assemble the finished product.

Frosting (for 2 logs)

- 3 squares of unsweetened chocolate
- 3 tablespoons of butter
- 4 tablespoons of hot coffee
- 2 cups of sifted powdered sugar

Melt the chocolate with the butter. Add half of the coffee to the sugar and stir into the chocolate, then add enough coffee to make the frosting soft enough to spread.

Meringue Mushrooms

- 2 egg whites
- ½ teaspoon of vanilla extract
- dash of salt
- ½ teaspoon of vinegar
- ¾ cup of sugar
- cocoa

Bring the egg whites to room temperature, then beat with the salt to stiff peaks. At low speed, add sugar gradually, beating a couple of minutes after each addition. Heat the oven to 275°. Add vinegar and vanilla to the mixture and beat three minutes at high speed. Put some of the mixture into a decorating tube. To make mushroom caps, squeeze out a blob and twist, filling ¾ of a buttered cookie sheet. For stems, squeeze more lightly, making columns. Bake 10 minutes, then turn the temperature to 250° and bake until the pieces are slightly golden. Remove from the pan and cool. Attach the stems to the caps with a dab of the frosting mix and dust the completed mushrooms with cocoa. They may be stored in a covered container until needed.

Assembly

Unroll the desired number of cakes and spread with the cream filling, then re-roll them. Put the filled, rolled logs end to end on a foil-covered board on which you have arranged clean pine boughs. Quickly frost the logs in a long line so that you appear to have one single log; leave the ends unfrosted. Attach the mushrooms while the frosting is still wet. Sift powdered sugar over the whole log and the pine boughs, like snow. Lay a knife next to the log so everyone can cut a piece and enjoy.

Miriam Gourley: Cosette's Doll

Color picture on page 63

I first met Miriam Gourley a decade ago, when I began selling her patterns to quilt stores. Her wonderful dolls are always very carefully researched for historical and cultural accuracy: in using her designs and instructions, you also learn about the society represented. In addition to her enormous talents and productivity in doll design, for her own as well as for other companies, she co-ordinates the annual Dollmakers Magic show, designs garments for the Fairfield fashion show, and has written a book on making cloth dolls. With all of the activity in her very busy professional and family life, this calm and competent lady graciously and enthusiastically agreed to make a doll for you in this book.

When my siblings and I were young, our mother often told us stories from classic novels: one of my favorites was from Victor Hugo's *Les Misérables*. Jean Valjean, the hero, came to rescue Cosette from the Thenadiers, greedy and cruel innkeepers, temporary guardians who kept her in rags and enslaved her. Jean brought her a beautiful doll, and I have tried to imagine it in creating this doll, even though hers was probably porcelain. Some of the fabrics and laces I used were tea-dyed, to give the appearance of age. I selected an elegant look, hoping that is what Cosette was given: bridal lace for sleeves and trimmings; silk petticoat edged with hand-crocheted antique lace; brocade ribbons and satin ribbon roses. The skirt is made from Christmas fabric, and she holds a wreath: Jean's kindness to Cosette exemplifies what Christmas should be.

SUPPLY LIST

- Head / Torso and Arms — ⅓ yard of unbleached muslin

- Legs — ½ yard of fabric to simulate stockings; Poly-fil® stuffing

- Sleeves — skirt fabric or 14" of 12"-wide scalloped lace

- Petticoat and Pantaloons — ½ yard of tea-dyed silk; ½ yard of 1"-wide lace; ⅔ yard of 3" to 4"-wide antique lace

- Bodice embellishment — ½ yard of ⅞"-wide cream brocade ribbon; ⅔ yard of 4"-wide lace; 6 ribbon roses (¼" wide)

- Skirt — ½ yard of a cotton print; ½ yard of 1⅜"-wide brocade satin ribbon for the top of the skirt and ⅔ yard for a waist tie; 6-8 ribbon roses (¼" wide)

- Embroidery floss for face — Anchor® #378, 0373, 0883, 100, 403, 860

- Hair — 1½ ounces of Earthspun deep red mohair

- Delta light brown Fabric Dye® for the shoes

- 3½ yards of ⅛"-wide silk ribbon, and ¼"-wide ribbon for additional embellishment

TOOLS

- Assorted sizes of dowels or other stuffing tools

- Embroidery needle

- Hot glue gun and glue sticks, or white tacky glue

- Thread to match fabrics

- Cotton swab to apply blush

- Floral wire

- Nippers or old scissors to cut wire

GENERAL INSTRUCTIONS

You will use a ¼" seam allowance throughout.

You may wish to tea-dye lace, fabric, and ribbons before you begin.

Finish all clothing seams by serging or by trimming them to ⅛" and zigzagging.

If you wish to embroider the face before cutting the pieces, trace the face and pattern shape onto the muslin, place in a hoop, and follow the embroidery instructions.

HEAD / TORSO

1. Cut out the head / torso and trace the face with a #2 pencil or a fine-tip permanent-ink marking pen.

2. Cut lace to fit across the torso, as indicated on the pattern. Stitch the lace to the torso.

3. Place the pieces right sides together and stitch around them, leaving the bottom open for turning. Reinforce the neck with a second stitching. Trim the seam allowance to ⅛" and clip the neck curves. Turn right sides out and stuff firmly, especially the head and neck. Baste the bottom closed to keep stuffing in.

4. Embroider the face in the following order. You may make knots at the back of the head, where the hair will cover them.

Eyelid	Anchor 0373 (Gold / Beige)	Satin stitch, 2 threads
Iris	Anchor 860 (Dull Green)	Satin stitch, 2 threads
Pupil	Anchor 403 (Black)	Satin stitch, 2 threads

Outline rounds of eyes; eyebrows and nose	Anchor 378 (Light Brown)	Outline stitch, 1 thread
Lips (top first)	Anchor 0883 (Coral)	Satin stitch, 2 threads

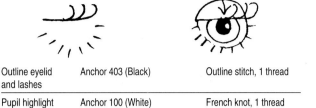

Outline eyelid and lashes	Anchor 403 (Black)	Outline stitch, 1 thread
Pupil highlight	Anchor 100 (White)	French knot, 1 thread wrapped 3 times

5. Apply powder blush with a cotton swab to add cheek color.

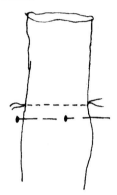

LEGS

1. Cut out the pieces, and mark the knee area and shoe line with a pencil.

2. Place the legs together, right sides together, and stitch around them, leaving the top open for turning. Trim the seam allowance to ⅛", turn them and stuff to within ½" of the knee line.

3. To facilitate top-stitching, place pins about ¼" below the knee line, as illustrated; this will enable the machine to stitch smoothly without the stuffing getting in the way. (Use the same technique for the elbows.) Top-stitch the knee, from one seam to the other.

4. Continue stuffing the leg firmly to within 1" of the top, and baste closed.

5. Paint the shoe with the fabric dye. Apply a second coat if necessary.

PANTALOONS

1. Zigzag the lower edge to finish the raw edges. Press under ½" and machine hem the lower edge. Baste the scalloped lace onto the hemmed edge of the pantaloon leg. Overlap the top edge of the lace with ½" brocade ribbon and top-stitch both edges of the ribbon. The scalloped edge will hang over the lower edge, as shown.

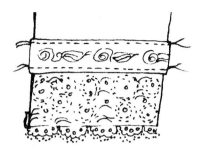

2. Fold each pantaloon leg in half, right sides together, matching lace and ribbon. Stitch the back seam and finish as indicated under General Instructions.

3. Turn each pantaloon leg right side out and press it.

4. Place the pantaloon leg on the doll leg, pantaloon seam at the back. Adjust the pantaloon length by trimming excess at the top. The lace should meet the top sides of the shoe, as shown. Center the leg inside the pantaloon and make a gathering stitch across the top through all layers.

5. Gather the legs to fit inside the lower edge of the torso (remove basting at torso bottom).

6. Place the front lower edge of the torso and the raw edges of the legs together and stitch them together. Do not stitch through the back of the torso. Fold ¼" of the torso back under and pin to the previously stitched torso and legs. Hand stitch the opening closed, covering all raw edges.

7. Tie a 1" bow of ¼" ribbon and tack to the center front, at the bottom edge of the brocade ribbon.

ARMS

1. Cut out the arms and mark the elbows and fingers with a pencil.

2. Place the pieces right sides together and stitch around them, leaving an opening in the upper side. Trim the seam allowance to ⅛" and clip between thumb and fingers, and the inside arm curve.

3. Turn right sides out and stuff the finger area lightly. Top-stitch the fingers and continue

stuffing to within ½" of the elbow. Top-stitch the arm with the front and back seams in the center of the arms, as shown. Finish stuffing to the top, and stitch the opening closed.

4. Tack the arm to the shoulder, using strong thread such as quilting thread.

SLEEVES

1. If you are using lace for the sleeves, place the bottom edge of the pattern on the scalloped edge of the lace (see the lace line on the pattern). If you use skirt fabric, zigzag the lower edge of the sleeve facing to finish the raw edge.

2. Place the sleeve pieces right sides together and stitch the side seams. Press them open.

3. If you used fabric, hem by folding the sleeve facing toward the inside of the sleeve. Blind-stitch the facing to the sleeve.

4. Attach the ½" ribbon to the top edge of the lace on the torso. Begin at the top of one sleeve and tack at 1" intervals, pulling the ribbon forward for a little fullness, and gathering tightly as illustrated. Continue completely around the upper torso.

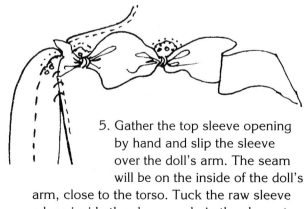

5. Gather the top sleeve opening by hand and slip the sleeve over the doll's arm. The seam will be on the inside of the doll's arm, close to the torso. Tuck the raw sleeve edges inside the sleeve and pin the sleeve to the body. Stitch at the shoulder and all around the arm.

6. Commercial ribbon roses often have loops of green ribbon for leaves. Trim the loops shorter by cutting at a 45° angle, as shown.

Use fabric glue, or stitch the roses to the gathered areas of the ribbon border.

Cut

PETTICOAT

1. Place the petticoat pieces right sides together and stitch the back seam (short edges) to within 2" of the top. Press the seam flat.

2. Zigzag the lower edge to finish the raw edges and press under a 1" hem. Blind-stitch the hem. Make a ½" tuck by measuring 1½" up from the hemmed edge. Using this as a fold line, fold the bottom edge toward the inside of the petticoat. Stitch ½" from the new edge and press the tuck down toward the hem.

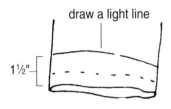

draw a light line

1½"

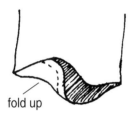

fold up

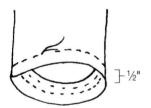

½"

3. Stitch the 3" antique lace by hand to the inside of the lower edge of the petticoat, seams in the back.

4. Place the petticoat on the doll. The bottom of the lace should meet the bottom edge of the pantaloon ribbon, and the top should be at the hip, not the waist. You may need to trim the top. Set the petticoat aside.

SKIRT

1. Trace the scalloped border onto lightweight cardboard to make a template, with which you will trace the scallops onto the lower edge of the skirt. Cut out the scallops.

2. Place the skirt pieces right sides together and stitch the back seam. Press flat.

3. Press under ¼" of one of the long edges of the skirt facing. Place the facing pieces right sides together and stitch the back seam. Press it and place the facing right sides together with the scalloped edge of the skirt, matching the back seams. The folded edge is toward the top of the scallops.

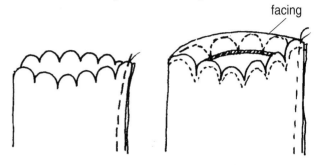

facing

4. Stitch ¼" from the edge of the scallops and clip between the curves. Turn the scallops right sides out and press. Blind-stitch the folded edge of the facing to the wrong side of the skirt. Turn the skirt right side out.

5. Gather the skirt and the petticoat, separately, to 11". Place the petticoat inside the skirt, matching the back seams. Be sure the lace edge shows below the skirt scallops.

6. Press under one of the long edges of the waistband and pin the band to the gathered edges of the skirt / petticoat, right sides together and matching raw edges. Stitch. Fold the raw ends of the waistband under ¼", as illustrated.

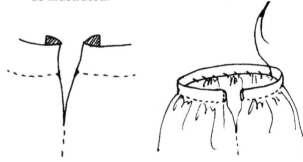

7. Fold the waistband over so the folded edge covers all the gathered edges. Stitch in place.

8. Place the skirt on the doll and adjust on the hips. The opening should be at the center back of the doll. Stitch the skirt to the doll and stitch the waistband together in the back, but do not stitch the skirt opening. This will be useful to hide the doll stand.

9. Attach 1⅜" ribbon to the waistband at 1" intervals, as you did with the torso, and embellish with ribbon streamers and roses. Streamers were made from ⅛"-wide silk ribbons, cut 6"-10" in length, folded in half, stitched in the center and tacked to the gathered sections of the wide ribbon.

10. Tie ⅔ yard of 1⅜" ribbon snugly around the waist and tie a bow in the back.

HAIR

1. The fiber I used is dyed mohair, which has natural curl that fills the head sumptuously. Sort through the package and find the smoothest, curliest, most tangle-free fibers. You may comb the ends of sections that need it, although you will remove some of the curl. To restore the curl, wet the fiber and let dry slowly.

2. Cut a 2" square of muslin. Place the fibers across the square, centering it. When you have enough fiber, longest lengths possible, stitch down the center as shown.

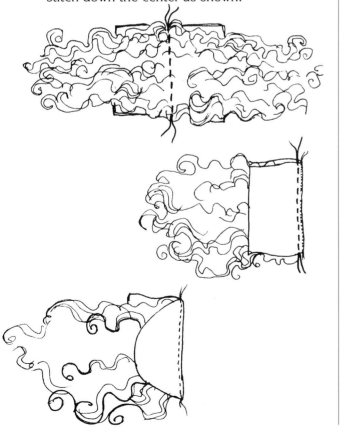

3. Fold the square along the stitch, mohair inside. Stitch as close as possibly to the folded edge, as illustrated.

4. Cut the muslin into a football shape, points at the ends of the stitch line.

5. Open the wig flat and pin it to the head, in the best position. Attach with either white tacky glue (can be re-positioned) or hot glue.

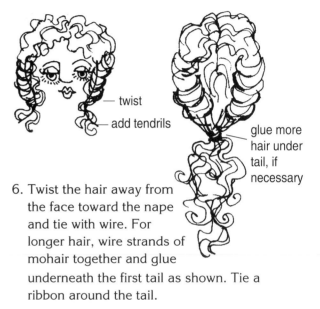

— twist
— add tendrils
glue more hair under tail, if necessary

6. Twist the hair away from the face toward the nape and tie with wire. For longer hair, wire strands of mohair together and glue underneath the first tail as shown. Tie a ribbon around the tail.

7. Select two strands of curly hair and glue underneath the hair at the temples, for a more romantic hair-do.

Christmas has always been my favorite holiday. With three sisters and four brothers, an allowance didn't go very far. I remember spending an average of 79¢ per gift, but I have fond memories of making those simple selections. When Bruce and I married, we started our Christmas traditions, with the primary focus on the religious meaning of the holiday; therefore, we try to make gifts which are extensions of ourselves. After Thanksgiving, I begin to help the children make gifts for cousins and friends — fabric motifs fused onto pillowcases; commercial craft panels stitched by me, stuffed by the children, then embellished and packaged; child-created cards and decorations, and holiday baking. I keep spices simmering on the stove during the season.

Bruce's parents dress as Mr. and Mrs. Santa for a department store and for family parties. On Christmas eve, after they have returned to grandparent clothes, their children and grandchildren meet at their house for a special supper and gift exchange. On Christmas morning in our own home, after Santa's gifts are surveyed, we have a traditional breakfast of green pancakes with whipped cream and strawberries. (We add a little green food coloring to the batter.) After our red and green breakfast, we open the presents we have exchanged with each other.

Since Christmas is also my birthday, we hold that celebration in the evening. We always have my favorite chocolate cake while I open my presents. I have never felt deprived by my birthdate: I have always felt rather lucky to have been born on such a special day. My mother always told me I was her best Christmas present!

Simmering Potpourri

Save the peels from oranges and lemons. Let them dry thoroughly and break them into small pieces, about ½" wide. Put about ¼ cup of citrus peels into simmering water. Add a bay leaf, 1 tablespoon of whole cloves, and a cinnamon stick. Add more water as necessary.

Layered Salad

Combine in a mixing bowl:

- 1 cup of Best Foods® or Hellman's® mayonnaise
- ½ cup of buttermilk
- Scant ¼ teaspoon each of salt, Ac´cent®, onion salt, garlic powder, pepper

Whisk together and add 3 cups of sour cream. Blend all together well and refrigerate.

Salad

- ½ head of lettuce
- 1 package of washed spinach leaves
- 2 cups of Swiss cheese, cubed
- 8 ounces of frozen green peas
- 2 bunches of green onions, chopped
- 1 pound of bacon, cooked crisp and chopped
- 6 hard-boiled eggs, sliced

Tear the lettuce and spinach into bite-size pieces. In a four-quart clear glass bowl, layer the lettuce, spinach, cheese, peas, and onions. Repeat until the salad is about 1" from the top of the bowl, or all ingredients have been used. Just before serving, top with bacon, egg slices, and three cups of the dressing.

SKIRT TEMPLATE

TEMPLATES

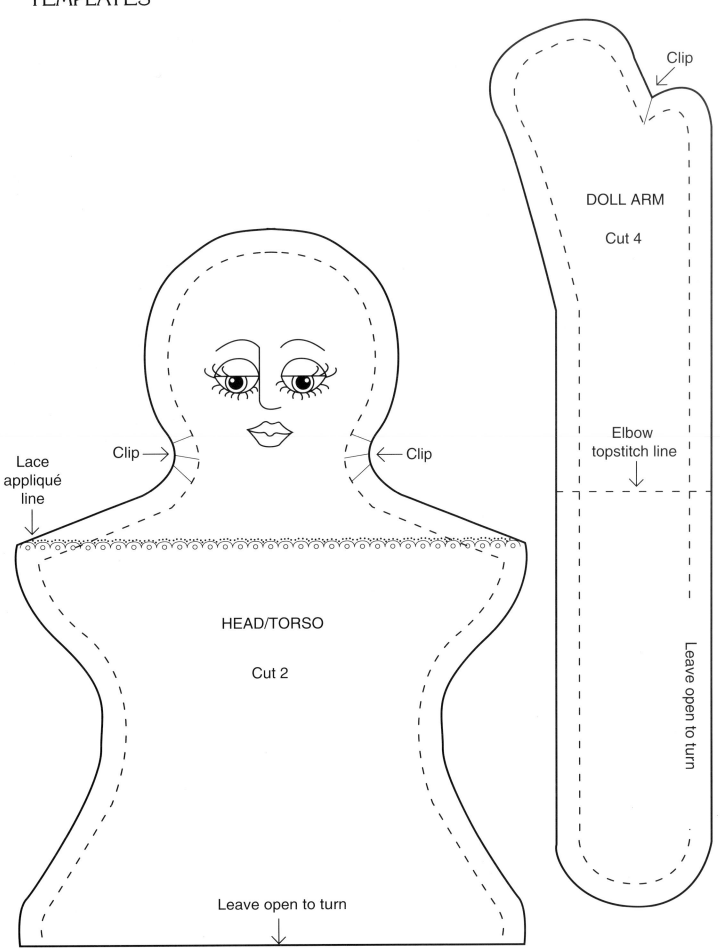

Lace
appliqué
line

Clip

Clip

HEAD/TORSO

Cut 2

Leave open to turn

Clip

DOLL ARM

Cut 4

Elbow
topstitch line

Leave open to turn

gather

SLEEVE

(Cut 2)

Cutting line for
scalloped lace edge

WAISTBAND (Cut 1)
$1\frac{3}{4}$" x 11"

SKIRT FACING (Cut 1)   2" X 24"

PANTALOON LEG (Cut 2)
$6\frac{1}{2}$" x 16"

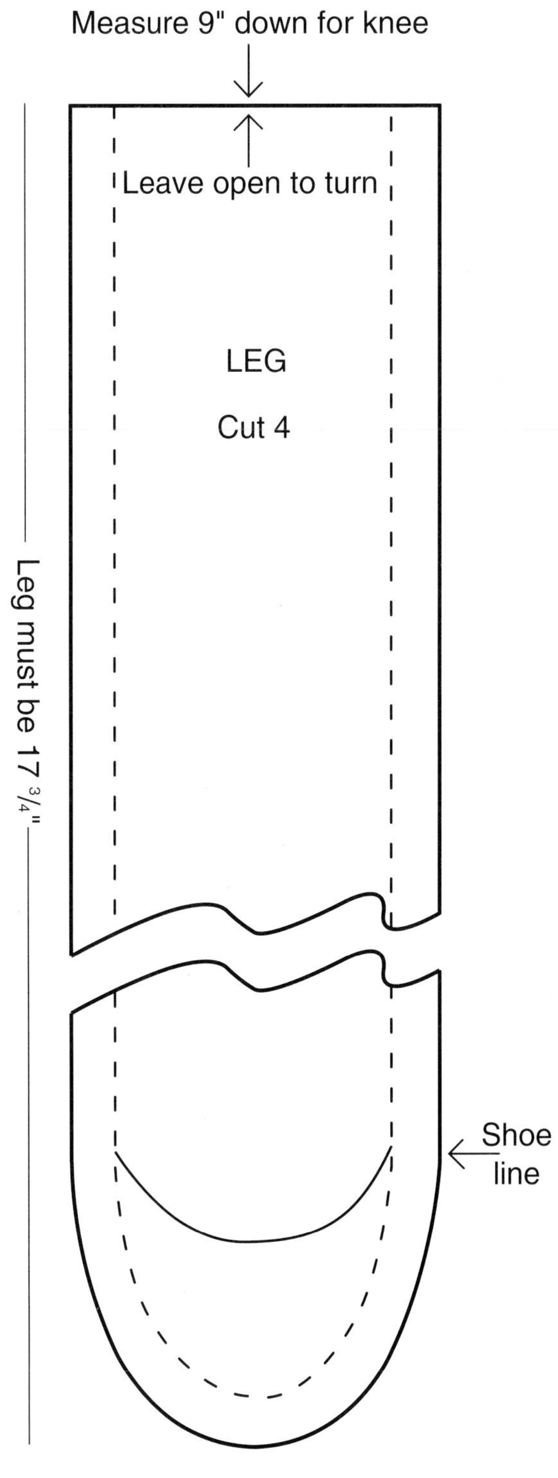

Measure 9" down for knee

Leave open to turn

LEG

Cut 4

Leg must be 17 $\frac{3}{4}$"

SKIRT (Cut 1)
$13\frac{1}{2}$" x 24"

PETTICOAT (Cut 1)
$14\frac{1}{2}$" x 22"

Shoe
line

MARGARET PETERS has been a craftswoman all her life. Her real involvement with fiber arts began in 1975, when she started to create needlepoint designs — and to win national awards for them. Teaching at and managing a needlepoint store, and then representing needlepoint and cross-stitch manufacturers, she attended trade shows; she became fascinated by the quilting she encountered and began representing quilting suppliers as well. Eventually, she carried the products of 75 pattern and fabric companies.

By the mid-1980's, she had also begun to design her own dolls, and was nationally known for her Christmas shows for her clients. These talents came together in 1987, when she was invited to design a Christmas tree for the Smithsonian Institution. She then started her own design and supply company, and she was asked to create dolls for Fairfield Processing and touring shows: Dollmakers Magic, Cut from the Same Cloth, Accessories as Art, etc. She began national touring herself, speaking especially to quilt and antique audiences — including three times at Quilt Market and Quilt Festival — about the Smithsonian experience, effective store displays, and Christmas. In 1991, she was invited by West Point Pepperell to design a promotion for their fabrics: she created Old Glory: Long May She Wave, the flag challenge which has toured the country.

Her home in Walnut Creek, California, is such a treasure trove of antiques, American crafts, patriotic memorabilia, and Christmas crafts that it receives media coverage regularly, it is used by book publishers for photographic settings, and it is the site of annual Christmas tours by various crafts organizations.

Margaret's line of roving for doll hair is marketed under the name Ewe and Me Roving; her American flags by the yard, angels and other Christmas ornaments are marketed as Long May She Wave. Both are available in your local craft shops. You may obtain further information and her catalogue from: Margaret Peters, Department H, 325 Lancaster Road, Walnut Creek, CA 94595.

Ac´cent is a registered trademark of Pet, Inc.
Aleene's Tacky Glue is a trademark of Aleene's Division, Artis, Inc.
Anchor is a registered trademark of Susan Bates, Inc.
Bernina 1230 is a registered trademark of Fritz Gegauf, Ltd.
Best Foods and Hellman's are registered trademarks of CPC International Inc.
Candlelight and Metallic 601 are trademarks of YLI.
Delta Fabric Dye is a registered trademark of Delta/Shiva.
Earthspun is a product of Thomas Enterprises.
Elna is a trademark of Elna Inc.
Ewe and Me is a registered trademark of Ewe and Me.
Mylar is a registered trademark of E. I. duPont de Nemours & Co.
New Home Memory Craft 7000 is a registered trademark of The New Home Sewing Machine Co.
Olfa is a registered trademark of Olfa Products Corp.
Pigma Micron is a registered trademark of the Sakura Color Products Corp. of America.
Pilot is a registered trademark of the Pilot Pen Corporation of America.
Poly-fil is a registered trademark of Fairfield Processing Corp.
Ribbon Thread is a trademark of Elna Inc.
Strathmore Blank Greeting Cards are a product of Strathmore Paper Co.
Sulky is a registered trademark of Sulky of America.
Super Sculpey is a registered trademark of Polyform Products Co.
Tombo Dual Brush-Pens are a product of Tombo.
Ultrasuede is a registered trademark of Springs Industries.
WonderUnder is a registered trademark of the Pellon Division, Freudenberg Nonwovens.

For further information about the mohair Miriam Gourley used, write to:

Earthspun Hair
Thomas Enterprises
P.O. Box 365
Lehi, UT 84043

Marinda Stewart's patterns are available from:

Marinda Stewart
P.O. Box 402 - Dept. P
Walnut Creek, CA 94596

Please enclose a stamped self-addressed envelope.

Sally Collins' designs can be ordered from her at:

Special Treasures
P.O. Box 30034 - Dept. P
Walnut Creek, CA 94598

For materials for Christmas cards:

YLI
482 North Freedom Boulevard
Provo, UT 84601
800-854-1932

Aardvark Adventures
P.O. Box 2449
Livermore, CA 94551
510-443-2687

Margaret's line of roving hair is available from:

Ewe and Me
325 Lancaster Road
Walnut Creek, CA 94595

Other Fine Quilting Books from C & T Publishing

An Amish Adventure, by Roberta Horton

Appliqué 12 Easy Ways!, by Elly Sienkiewicz

Art of Silk Ribbon Embroidery, by Judith Montano

Baltimore Album Quilts, Historic Notes and Antique Patterns, by Elly Sienkiewicz

Baltimore Beauties and Beyond, (3 volumes), by Elly Sienkiewicz

Boston Commons Quilt, by Blanche Young and Helen Young Frost

Calico and Beyond, by Roberta Horton

A Celebration of Hearts, by Jean Wells and Marina Anderson

Crazy Quilt Handbook, by Judith Montano

Crazy Quilt Odyssey, by Judith Montano

Crosspatch, by Pepper Cory

Dimensional Appliqué, Baskets, Blooms and Baltimore Borders, by Elly Sienkiewicz

Fans, by Jean Wells

Fine Feathers, by Marianne Fons

Flying Geese Quilt, by Blanche Young and Helen Young Frost

Friendship's Offering, by Susan McKelvey

Happy Trails, by Pepper Cory

Heirloom Machine Quilting, by Harriet Hargrave

Imagery on Fabric, by Jean Ray Laury

Irish Chain Quilt, by Blanche Young and Helen Young Frost

Isometric Perspective, by Katie Pasquini-Masopust

Landscapes & Illusions, by Joen Wolfrom

Let's Make Waves, by Marianne Fons and Liz Porter

Light and Shadows, by Susan McKelvey

Magical Effects of Color, by Joen Wolfrom

Mandala, by Katie Pasquini

Mariner's Compass, by Judy Mathieson

Mastering Machine Appliqué, by Harriet Hargrave

Memorabilia Quilting, by Jean Wells

New Lone Star Handbook, by Blanche Young and Helen Young Frost

Patchwork Quilts Made Easy: The Milky Way Quilt, by Jean Wells

Patchwork Quilts Made Easy: The Nine-Patch Quilt, by Jean Wells

Patchwork Quilts Made Easy: The Pinwheel Quilt, by Jean Wells

Patchwork Quilts Made Easy: The Stars & Hearts Quilt, by Jean Wells

Perfect Pineapples, by Jane Hall and Dixie Haywood

Picture This, by Jean Wells and Marina Anderson

Plaids and Stripes, by Roberta Horton

Quilting Designs from the Amish, by Pepper Cory

Quilting Designs from Antique Quilts, by Pepper Cory

Story Quilts, by Mary Mashuta

3 Dimensional Design, by Katie Pasquini

Trip Around the World Quilts, by Blanche Young and Helen Young Frost

Visions: The Art of the Quilt, by Quilt San Diego

Visions: Quilts of a New Decade, by Quilt San Diego

Wearable Art for Real People, by Mary Mashuta

Working in Miniature, by Becky Schaefer

For more information, write for a free catalog:

C & T Publishing

P.O. Box 1456

Lafayette, CA 94549